Fan Translations

Fan Translations

JONATHAN EVANS
AND TING GUO

BLOOMSBURY ACADEMIC
NEW YORK • LONDON • OXFORD • NEW DELHI • SYDNEY

BLOOMSBURY ACADEMIC
Bloomsbury Publishing Inc, 1359 Broadway, New York, NY 10018, USA
Bloomsbury Publishing Plc, 50 Bedford Square, London, WC1B 3DP, UK
Bloomsbury Publishing Ireland, 29 Earlsfort Terrace, Dublin 2, D02 AY28, Ireland

BLOOMSBURY, BLOOMSBURY ACADEMIC and the Diana logo are trademarks of
Bloomsbury Publishing Plc

First published in the United States of America 2026

Cover design: Eleanor Rose
Cover image © London Games Festival, Video Game Cosplay Character Parade through
London, UK, 14 April 2018. Photograph © Jeff Gilbert / Alamy

Library of Congress Cataloging-in-Publication Data
Names: Evans, Jonathan (Senior lecturer in translation studies) author |
Guo, Ting author
Title: Fan translations / Jonathan Evans and Ting Guo.
Description: New York : Bloomsbury Academic, 2026. | Series: Bloomsbury
fandom primers | Includes bibliographical references and index.
Identifiers: LCCN 2025024752 | ISBN 9798765113653 hardback |
ISBN 9798765113691 paperback | ISBN 9798765113677 pdf |
ISBN 9798765113660 epub
Subjects: LCSH: Translating and interpreting in mass media | Translating
and interpreting–Social aspects | Fans (Persons) | Reader-response criticism
Classification: LCC P96.T83 E83 2026 | DDC 418/.02–dc23/eng/20250523
LC record available at https://lccn.loc.gov/2025024752

ISBN: HB: 979-8-7651-1365-3
PB: 979-8-7651-1369-1
ePDF: 979-8-7651-1367-7
eBook: 979-8-7651-1366-0

Series: Bloomsbury Fandom Primers

Typeset by Deanta Global Publishing Services, Chennai, India
Printed and bound in the United States of America

For product safety related questions contact productsafety@bloomsbury.com.

To find out more about our authors and books visit www.bloomsbury.com and
sign up for our newsletters.

CONTENTS

ACKNOWLEDGMENTS

Thanks to Paul Booth and Rukmini Pande for asking us to propose this volume for the Fandom Primers series. We appreciate an interest in fan translation from outside of translation studies! Thanks to the team at Bloomsbury, especially Stephanie Grace-Petinos and Katie Gallof Houck, for all their support. Our anonymous reviewers provided useful suggestions and welcome enthusiasm for the project.

Susan Bassnett, Olga Castro, Ernesto Priego, and Jamie Jing Zhao read parts of the manuscript and provided helpful feedback. We understand how difficult it is to find time for such things in packed academic workloads, so we are doubly appreciative.

Many people have encouraged us to work on fan translations, sometimes indirectly, for which we are grateful: Brian Baer, Mona Baker, Hongwei Bao, Hélène Buzelin, Tessa Dwyer, Lincoln Geraghty, Tianji Guo, Matt Hills, Henry Jones, Cristina Marinetti, Chris Mellinger, Lori Morimoto, David Orrego-Carmona, Luis Pérez-González, Jan Pedersen, Douglas Robinson, Gabriela Saldanha, Dingkun Wang, and no doubt many others whom we have spoken to about the topic. We've appreciated presenting on fandom and translation at conferences and talks in Norwich, Seville, Brighton, Ho Chi Minh City, Shenzhen, Hong Kong, and as part of the Nida School of Translation Studies in Misano Adriatico. Our thanks to the organizers and audiences at those events.

Jonathan Evans would like to thank Greater Glasgow and Clyde NHS for treatment, some of which overlapped with writing this book; the University of Glasgow for providing research leave in which to write my portion of the book; colleagues in Comparative Literature and Translation Studies at

Glasgow for covering my research leave (especially Magdalena Kampert, Yifei Kong, and Vera Mengxue Zhao), and for conversations on translation and other topics (especially Susan Bassnett, Shanti Graheli, and Michael Syrotinski). My PhD students have made me keep up to date and challenged my thinking in some useful ways. The seed of this project started while I was still working at Portsmouth, and I must thank the Faculty of Humanities and Social Sciences for funding projects that led me to work more on this topic and Akiko Sakamoto for being my critical buddy. Thanks to former collaborators on fan translation, Laura Macdonald and Van Nhan Luong, as well as current collaborators Jinsil Choi, Mattea Cussel, Fruela Fernández, and Kyunghye Kim. Thanks to the British Academy, the Newton Fund, the Fund for International Collaboration, the ESRC, and the AHRC for funding projects adjacent to the current one. Rowan has shared her fandoms with us endlessly, and it's been a joy to watch (though not necessarily hear). Rory has shown us how early media preferences start and forced me to have a healthier work-life balance.

Ting Guo would like to thank the AHRC and the University of Liverpool for providing funding to support projects that have deepened my thinking on this topic and colleagues in the Department of Languages, Cultures, and Film at Liverpool for welcoming me to Liverpool and supporting me throughout Jon's treatment when this book was written. Particular thanks go to Aiqing Wang, Liehui Wang, and Lei Peng for covering my teaching, Claire Taylor and Soumyen Bandyopadhyay for providing constructive feedback on various applications. Outside the academy, my research related to this book has been inspired and supported by many international, especially Chinese, individual fans and fan groups. I am enormously grateful for the support and advice offered by each of them. I can't list all of their names here, but I'd particularly like to thank my friends from Jihua Network, Aibai, and QAFone. Finally, special thanks to my family for all the love and support.

CHAPTER ONE

What Are Fandom and Translation?

Let's start thinking about fan translation with a classic example, quoted from Henry Jenkins's *Textual Poachers* (1992, 76), a pioneering text in fan studies. At a *Beauty and the Beast* fan club meeting, they are watching episodes in French that had been recorded from a broadcast in Canada, but which had not aired in the United States:

> Here, mutual assistance was required to decipher the narrative content as none of the members was fluent in French. The members were encouraged to "shout out" if they could make sense of any of the words from their limited exposure to French in college or high school . . .

This chaotic-sounding situation brings up multiple, interconnected aspects of fan translation. The first is that fans of a series or object will go beyond their own language in order to find out more or to watch episodes that they would otherwise not have access to. Fans may even be fans of a TV show or music in another language entirely and learn that language to engage better with the object of their fandom; this is often the case for K-pop fans, for example (Pickles 2018). Second, fan translations are inherently part of the fan community and seldom done solely for someone's own personal pleasure or experience, but rather to share an object, an experience, or an interpretation. Jenkins remarks on how fandom is connected to public "retellings" and sharing information with other fans (Jenkins 1992, 77). Third, fan translations can overcome market logics and existing flows of media products: here, from Quebecois French into English, although it was an American TV show to begin with.

It is interesting that the anecdote that Jenkins uses here relates to French, which, it can be assumed, many English-speaking readers in the United Kingdom and the United States have learned some of throughout their education. It would read as quite a different anecdote if the TV show was in Spanish, given the demographic makeup of the United States and the likelihood that there would be some Spanish native speakers in the group. It would be equally different if the show was in Japanese or Korean, though Jenkins does note that anime clubs (of the 1980s) also had similar practices (1992, 76). Yet it would also have a different feel to it if the TV show was in English and the audience were somewhere else in the world, such as China, given the prevalence of English learning the world over, and the often central role of English-language, specifically North American, media production in the global mediasphere.

A simple anecdote like this, which sounds like a fun event, if a rather unhelpful way of watching a TV show, highlights the connection of fan translation with some bigger issues. One of these issues is language hierarchies; that is, the comparative power of different languages and how this affects how they are perceived around the world. Another is global cultural flows and how these are influenced by consumers. Third, the role that fans play in the formation of global media culture. These in turn lead to questions of cosmopolitanism, intercultural communication, and individual agency in a corporate world. It's this connectedness to wider questions that makes fan translations so rewarding to study.

This book is the first monograph to study fan translations as a phenomenon. They have been studied in articles and book chapters previously—we will come back to the scholarship on the topic in Chapter 2—but there has not been a single book that focused on the topic. We aim this book at readers in both media studies and translation studies, as well as the humanities and social sciences more generally. This means that we will assume very little knowledge of the topic or scholarship in order to be as accessible as we can be to the widest audience.

We present this book as an important point of reference for new readers, but we also plan to offer new readings and discussions that will move the field on and open up new paths for scholarship. These agenda-setting interventions will come mainly in Chapters 3, 4, and 5, which focus on post- and de-colonial fandoms, queer fandoms, and the effect of fan translation on professional translation and media distribution practices. The nature of the Fandom Primers series as short books means that it is impossible to cover every aspect of fan translation and that the examples we discuss are, of necessity, quite short. They serve to illustrate the arguments of the chapters rather than being fully formed case studies in their own right (though we hope that they inspire interested readers to undertake similar case studies).

Overall, *Fan Translations* argues for translation as a transformative fan practice that ought to be studied alongside other fan practices in the increasingly digitalized and transcultural fan culture. To demonstrate this, Chapter 2 gives an overview of fan translation as a phenomenon, exploring what sorts of texts get translated by fans and the legal issues around fan translation while suggesting future directions for research. Chapter 3 examines how fan studies often focus on practices undertaken by English-language fans and argues that more work needs to be done on fans working in other languages and outside the Global North, where translation can be a significant part of fans' interaction with media texts. Chapter 4 examines how translation of queer texts can form part of international LGBTQIA+ solidarity and help fans navigate ideas coming from other cultures. Chapter 5 serves as a conclusion and analyzes the impact of fan translations on the translation and media industries, looking at the example of *danmaku* as a means streaming platforms have used to engage audiences that also allows for translational engagement. Before we get into those questions, though, we need to begin with some basics: what is a fan and what is translation?

What's a Fan?

This question always feels like it should be simple. Fans are ... fans of something. But what does that mean? What are fannish relationships with texts or objects? What do fans do? Am I a fan of *Star Trek: The Next Generation* because I like watching it? Partly. Consumption is the start of fandom, as is, arguably, enjoyment. We become fans of something because we like that thing. But fandom is more than this.

Fandom and the question of what a fan is have long been debated within fan and media studies. A relatively influential and early definition can be found in John Fiske's *Understanding Popular Culture* (1989, 146–7): "Being a fan involves active, enthusiastic, partisan, participatory engagement with the text." These adjectives need a bit of unpacking: a fan is an active reader who makes meaning out of cultural texts rather than a passive consumer. They are enthusiastic about consuming those texts, that is, they enjoy them and voluntarily consume more. They are partisan: this means that they have preferences that they follow. Classic examples include being either a *Star Trek* or a *Star Wars* fan, or in the height of the console wars, playing a Nintendo or a Sega. There is, of course, no reason why you couldn't like both sides of those binaries, and from the perspective of popular culture in 2024 (when we are writing this), it seems a bit odd that someone would see these as either/or options. However, Fiske was writing in the late 1980s, and at the time this sort of discernment was common. His point is that fans are actively involved in creating such oppositions. Finally, the term "participatory" here means that fans are somehow creating something with the texts and making themselves producers. This point is contentious, and other scholars, as we shall see, are more uncertain about it. Fiske includes fan "gossip" (1989, 147) as an example of that productivity; in other words, fans like to talk to other people about the things they are fans of. Gossip is quite ephemeral, but it is a form of participation in a culture around a text. There are other fan activities that are more easily recorded as the productive outputs of fandom, such as fan criticism, fan fiction, cosplay, collecting, and fan tourism. Fiske summarizes his point by arguing that fans are discriminating and productive (ibid.), in other words, they choose certain texts over others and create something from them.

A more community-focused definition of fans and fandom can be found in Jenkins's *Textual Poachers*. He argues that media fandom consists of five dimensions:

> Its relationship to a particular mode of reception; its role in encouraging viewer activism; its function as an interpretive community; its particular traditions of cultural production; its status as an alternative social community. (Jenkins 1992, 1–2)

Where Fiske argued that fandom was a type of readerly engagement, Jenkins makes clear the social nature of fandom. He does begin with a mode of reception, but this is framed within an interpretive community, that is, a community of readers who agree on ways to interpret texts (Fish 1982). Jenkins further links this to social community of fans. It is not clear that all fans would easily agree with these terms, though. What if I consider myself a fan of something that does not connect me to a community? For example, one of the authors of this book thinks of themselves as a fan of the Japanese rock band Coaltar of the Deepers (COTD), but their only experience of the band has been listening to them on YouTube without feeling connected to a community of COTD fans around the world. Jenkins was working on specific groups of media fans in the late 1980s, which he was both a part of and observed, so his description fits those fans and their historical moment.

Another specific culture that has been explored is the otaku culture in Japan, that is, fans of the connected worlds of video gaming, animation, comic books, and science fiction films (normally coming from Japan). Hiroki Azuma notes that there are several hundred thousand otakus, with the qualifying statement: "And that's just counting those active otaku consumers who buy and sell derivative works or take part in cosplay, that is, dressing up in costumes to resemble characters from manga and anime" (Azuma 2009, 3–4). Like Jenkins, Azuma identifies active fans with the creation of derivative works or social activities like cosplay. However, he leaves a space to consider fans who are not actively involved in those cultures, who are less visible. Ideas about discernment become more complex in Azuma's work, which focuses on how otaku/fans consume media texts: for Azuma, they do not distinguish between original works and fan productions (2009, 26, 39). Again, Azuma is referring to one specific group of fans, and his conclusion cannot be generalized to all fans.

This sort of focus on one specific group or another is explainable by the fact that studies must have a scope, and if someone intends to do ethnography—which can be time-consuming and expensive to do—then they have to choose a specific group to focus on. However, as Matt Hills (2002, 2) has observed, this focus on individual fan cultures can separate them from the wider media and cultural context, as well as the complexity of interactions between fans' different interests. For example, being a fan of underground pop music could interact with a fandom of Japanese comics in the connections between the 1990s Glaswegian band Urusei Yatsura and the 1980s Japanese comic *Urusei Yatsura* by Rumiko Takahashi. In another example, Sonic Youth album covers of the late 1980s and early 1990s, by contemporary artists such as Gerhard Richter, Raymond Pettibon, and Mike Kelley, could lead to a fandom of contemporary art. Focusing on a single group of fans also tends to limit the definition of fan and fan activities to those performed by that group. Not all fans cosplay, for instance, but if you only looked at fans who did cosplay, then it would seem to be a trait of all fans.

A definition of fans needs to take these elements into account. Cornel Sandvoss offers one that tries to cover all fans: "I define fandom as the regular, emotionally involved consumption of a given popular narrative or text" (Sandvoss 2005, 8). There's a lot to commend in this definition: it doesn't distinguish between sports, media, and music fans. It highlights the affective aspect of fandom: fans are "emotionally involved" with the texts or things they are fans of. It also brings to the fore that this consumption is regular, that is, repeated and often. Fans don't just watch something once, they keep watching it. These elements are similar to what we have seen in the other theories we have discussed. More subtle is that "popular," which Sandvoss includes to qualify the texts. Given that the majority of scholarship on fans focuses on fans of popular genres, and to an extent fan studies developed out of studies of popular culture, this does make sense. However, it excludes fans of more "highbrow" genres. Yet there is work on fans of classical music (e.g., Prieto-Rodríguez and Fernández-Blanco 2000) and on fans of Chekhov (Tulloch 2007). Alan McKee (2007) and Matt Hills (2005, 150–73) have even argued that there are fans of cultural and literary theory, which is not really a "popular" discourse and requires an investment of time, effort, and money (for course fees) to be able to understand fully. More complicatedly, it is no longer entirely clear where the boundary lies between "popular" and "high" culture, or if there is one. A literature scholar like Sianne Ngai is equally at home writing about the TV show *I Love Lucy* (1951–7) as she is about the philosophers G. W. F. Hegel or Theodor Adorno in her *Our Aesthetic Categories* (2012). In a recent chapter analyzing attunement as an aesthetic response, literary critic Rita Felski uses examples that relate to the music of Joni Mitchell, a novel by Kazuo Ishiguro, a painting by Henri Matisse, Andrey Tarkovsky's film *Stalker*, and paintings by the seventeenth-century painter Nicolas Poussin (Felski 2020, 41–78). These examples span what would once have been the range from "popular" to "high" culture, yet Felski explores the same sorts of aesthetic responses, which echo the emotionally involved consumption that Sandvoss mentions, in all of them. It seems to us, then, that fandom is not limited to popular culture, even if studies of fandom have taken fans of popular culture as typical of fandom. To paraphrase Sandvoss, fandom involves regular, emotionally involved consumption of a text or group of texts (in the widest sense of what can be a text).

One final way in which fandom has been defined is to not define it explicitly but to assume that it has already been defined in practice. This approach is taken by Paul Booth and Lucy Bennett in their introduction to *Seeing Fans* (Booth and Bennett 2016). Instead of entering into discussions of what a fan is, they posit two approaches: fans as seen by fans, which includes a great deal of work within academic fan studies, and fans as seen by nonfans, which tends toward the portrayal of excessive behavior that early fan studies work was reacting against (e.g., Jenkins 1992, 9–49). While we think that this binary is itself reductive—some representations of fans by fans can in fact be quite negative, and others by nonfans can be more accommodating—the process of not setting out a definition but looking at how the term fan is used brings to mind Wittgenstein's contention that "the meaning of a word is its use in language" (Wittgenstein 1958, 20, §43). In other words, the way in which a word is regularly used in speech or writing gives it the sense that it has, rather than any theorizing about the semantics of it. So while fandom might well have a historical connection to the term "fanatic" (Jenkins 1992, 12), very seldom is it used in this sense anymore. This is partially because, as Booth and Bennett note, it is "no longer 'weird' to be a fan" (2016, 2): fandom has become far more mainstream around the world. People self-identify as fans much more easily than they did in the late 1980s, the period that Jenkins was studying. Not defining fandom theoretically but using it as a term defined by practice and existing work allows researchers to consider all sorts of fandom practices, from sports fans to classical music fans, as fandom, without reference to seemingly defining aspects such as popular culture or productivity.

In this book, we don't go quite as far as Booth and Bennett. Our understanding is that fans are typically emotionally involved in the things they are fans of and would also typically regularly consume (read, play, watch) those texts, understood in the widest sense, as in Sandvoss's definition that we have already discussed. This allows us to discuss people who are emotionally involved, regular consumers who may produce something (from gossip to derivative works) as fans even if they themselves might not use this term. For example, the board gamers we discuss in Chapter 4 exhibit many qualities of fans but don't necessarily see themselves as "fans" of board games.

Importantly, many of the fans that we discuss are actively involved in producing something: translations.

What's Translation?

When we first started presenting our work on fan translation at fan and film studies conferences, about ten years ago now, we were often confronted by other scholars saying something along the lines of, "we didn't know you could study that!" or "we didn't know translation was a productive practice." The fact that this book is in a series of Fandom Primers shows that attitudes are changing, but this experience made us realize that translation is not always understood as the complex process that we see it as. Indeed, just like the term "fan," once you scratch the surface, the term "translation" turns out to be not obvious in its meanings.

One definition that has been very influential and which highlights different types of translations is Roman Jakobson's tripartite definition of translation from 1959 (reprinted as Jakobson 2012). This is worth quoting in full:

1. Intralingual translation or *rewording* is an interpretation of verbal signs by means of other signs in the same language.
2. Interlingual translation or *translation proper* is an interpretation of verbal signs by means of some other language.
3. Intersemiotic translation or *transmutation* is an interpretation of verbal signs by means of signs of nonverbal sign systems.

(Jakobson 2012, 127; original emphasis)

Intralingual translation, the first category, is translation within the same language. This could be a summary of a longer text or a rephrasing of an utterance. Slightly more complicatedly, it could also mean subtitling for the Deaf and hard of hearing, which would normally take place in the same language, although here you also have a change from speech to writing in the form of subtitles, and subtitling for the Deaf and hard of hearing also tends to add some verbal representations of sounds (e.g., "Bangs the door"), which goes beyond a strict definition of intralingual translation. Intralingual translation can also include the changes made in editions of literary works for a British or American audience, as has been discussed by Linda Pillière (2021): here works such as the Harry Potter series have a number of minor changes made to make them more accessible for American children. For example, "rubbish" might be replaced by "trash." There are also changes in punctuation and spelling between American and British English. However, as Pillière notes, the changes often go beyond this. Indeed, in the case of David Mitchell's novel *Cloud Atlas* (2004), Martin Paul Eve (2016) has identified significant textual differences in its UK and US versions that affect the meaning of the text. More recent interest in the different possibilities of intralingual translation can be seen in the variety of topics in the *Routledge Handbook of Intralingual Translation* (Pillière and Berk Albachten 2024), which range from modernization to intralingual translation for different language varieties.

Jakobson's third category is intersemiotic translation. Following his phrasing, this could be any type of adaptation of a verbal text by something nonverbal. Any film adaptation of a novel would thus be intersemiotic translation, as would an illustration of a scene from a story, or even, arguably, a stop sign as it translates the word "Stop" into a symbol. There has been a lot written on the intersection between translation and adaptation (e.g., Hutcheon 2006; Raw 2012; Chan 2012; Milton and Cobelo 2023), and the borders between the two can be rather porous or ill-defined at times. While Jakobson only talks about the translation of verbal content by nonverbal signs, there is no reason that intersemiotic translation could not go the other way, that is, the translation of nonverbal signs by verbal ones. An obvious example of this would be the novelization of films, which has received little academic attention (an exception is Baetens 2018), or the smaller-level description of films or scenes from films that you would find in critical articles on film. Another example would be writing about visual images, known as ekphrasis, which has been studied much more extensively (recent examples include Kennedy and Meek 2018; Baugher 2020), or writing about music, which Elvis Costello famously compared to "dancing about architecture" (cited in Fabian 2015, 1), and which forms the basis of much music criticism and musicology. In fact, words do not have to be present at all, and you can imagine intersemiotic translations from film into music or music into images. Merchandising could arguably be a form of intersemiotic translation, as, for example, a film is expressed in plastic toys. Any time one sign system is represented by another could be a form of intersemiotic translation.[1]

This leaves the second of Jakobson's definitions: interlingual translation, which he confusingly calls "translation proper." Confusingly, as it seems to be a form of begging the question: interlingual translation is defined as translation. We will put aside the theoretical problems of this (as discussed by

Jacques Derrida (1992, 225), among others), as Jakobson's formulation could be seen as referring to what he perceives to be a common understanding of "translation": (interlingual) translation is the rewriting of a text in one language as a text in another language. This is what most people who are professional translators do. This is what we think of when we say we have read a translation of a literary text. An example of interlingual translation might be Lydia Davis's translation of Flaubert's *Madame Bovary* (Flaubert 2011), which is an English-language translation of the novel originally written in French. Translations are often thought of as book length, but could also be shorter fragments as quotes in other pieces of writing (as is common in academic writing, for instance). It could also refer to the interlingual subtitling of film and TV, which is between languages but which also moves from a spoken medium to a written one. Henrik Gottlieb (1994) has called subtitling "diagonal translation" for this reason. Film dubbing is also a form of interlingual translation, which stays within the same medium of speech, though it requires a script to be written and performed as part of the process. There are other forms of interlingual translation, such as the localization of software (e.g., Pym 2004), which, like subtitling, go beyond just representing a verbal text with one in another language, including other adaptations in terms of imagery or design. We think of interlingual translation as incorporating any translation of a text between languages, including ones that go beyond Jakobson's definition.[2]

In this book, we focus on *interlingual translation*, that is, translation across languages. As such, we are interested in how fans translate texts from one language to another, including how they might subtitle or dub film or television texts. While there are many instances of fans' transformational or derivative works that might in some sense be part of the wider definition of translation, from filking (songs about fan objects; Jenkins 1992, 250–76) to other fan-made paratexts (Gray 2010, 143–74) such as fan art or fan remixes, our focus on interlingual translation keeps in sight the aspect of translation across languages and the cross-linguistic and cross-cultural nature of much fandom, as well as fitting in with established understandings of fan translation, which we will return to in the next chapter.

However, we do not view translation as solely a linguistic phenomenon: it is connected to wider cultural behaviors and is embedded in culture as much as it is in language. Scholars such as Susan Bassnett and André Lefevere (1998) have argued that translation constructs cultures through its representation of them.[3] Any interlingual translation will have to deal with the fact that different languages (and sometimes different variants of those languages) are embedded in different cultural situations and may not have terms for certain items or practices. For example, the Scottish dish "stovies" proves difficult to translate, as it only really exists within Scotland and so doesn't have a standard translation into other languages. An explanation of it—potatoes boiled in meat stock until soft with some meat and onions mixed in—lacks any of the emotional connotations that stovies might have for someone living in Scotland, especially on a cold, dreich, gray afternoon. This is a relatively simple example of a foodstuff, but it demonstrates some of the cultural issues around translation that would equally affect more abstract concepts. Translation is also affected by external factors such as patronage (who pays for it), poetics (the existing norms and practices for that sort of text), and ideology (the underlying ideas about the world that are often expressed unconsciously), as Lefevere (1992) argues. Translation is, therefore, not just a straightforward transfer from one language to another but a recreation that is affected by many different factors.

What makes translation interesting is not, then, how it reproduces the original text (called the source text in translation studies), but rather the differences and discrepancies that appear, almost unavoidably, as part of the process of translation. As Bassnett has argued, "no translation can ever be the same as its original" (2014, 176), and as such, there is always some element of difference between the two texts.

Understanding this difference and explaining it lies at the core of translation analysis, though phrased like this it seems as if it should be simple to do, when it really isn't: it involves not only close analysis of the texts themselves but also the contexts in which they are produced and received. There is a human agency in translation that leads to such changes and which is, really, the important and central element of any attempt to analyze or interpret translation practices.

In fan studies terms, we are arguing that translation is a transformative work both shaped by the translator's own interpretation and which shapes the interpretation and reception of the original text and individual fans' experiences of being part of fan communities. While the transformations may differ in scale from those seen in fanfic or fan art, given the expectation that translation will represent the original text, translation remains on a continuum of adaptation (Hutcheon 2006) that includes other reworkings. As such, translation is just as much a part of fan activities as other (re) creative practices.

We have elsewhere (Guo and Evans 2020) argued that there is a "translational fandom," that is, a fandom where translating forms a significant part of fans' practices. This might be due to fans accessing material in languages other than their own and wanting to explore areas that have not been officially translated (as was the case of the Chinese group we studied in that article), or there may be other reasons. The intensity and frequency of fans' translation practices are likely to vary by context, but they constitute an important part of fans' experience of engaging with their favorite texts and being members of the communities. In the next chapter, we explore the existing work on fan translations to see what sorts of discussions already exist about this topic.

CHAPTER TWO

What Is Fan Translation?

Given the difficulties we saw in defining fans and translation in the previous chapter, it should come as no surprise that the topic of fan translation has also been approached from different angles within the discipline of translation studies. An example of this can be seen in the fact that fan translation gets two entries in the third edition of the *Routledge Encyclopedia of Translation Studies*: the first of these is titled "Fan audiovisual translation" (Pérez-González 2020) and the second is called "Fan translation" (Evans 2020a). While the first of these topics, focusing on practices such as fan subtitling (commonly known as *fansubbing*) and fan dubbing, would seem to be a subcategory of fan translation more widely, the splitting of these entries is indicative of the division of work being undertaken on fan translation: it tends to focus either on the translation of audiovisual media or some other genres of text. This holds as you look into the two entries: Luis Pérez-González focuses on subtitling and dubbing, while Jonathan Evans focuses on the translation of comics (known as *scanlation*), video game fan translation (known as *romhacking*), and more emergent practices such as the fan translation of songs and popular fiction.[1] There is also a slight difference in theoretical focus, with Pérez-González positioning fan audiovisual translation within a framework of "co-creative labor," drawing from work on labor in the cultural industries (see Banks and Deuze 2009), while Evans positions fan translation more clearly within fandom and fan studies. On the surface, these approaches may appear to differ, but they are actually quite complementary, and understanding fan translation as a form of fan labor (Deuze et al. 2007) can help to develop more critical approaches to fan practices that go beyond the more celebratory tones of earlier fan studies scholarship.

What we plan to do in the following two sections is to give an overview of scholarship on fan translation, charting how its foci have changed. While all practices of fan translation are of interest here, to make the discussion easier to follow, we will, like the *Routledge Encyclopedia of Translation Studies*, divide it by genres. We then come back to the overarching issue of copyright, which affects all genres, before suggesting future directions for thinking about fan translation as a transformative fan activity.

Before looking at the scholarship on fan translation in specific genres, it is worth pondering the name, *fan translation*. This implies a certain approach to translation and the people who do it. As Evans (2020a, 177) notes, "Fan translation is undertaken by fans." This may seem like a tautology, but it serves the purpose of separating fan translation from other forms of nonprofessional or unpaid translation, of which there are many (Pérez-González and Susam-Saraeva 2012), including pro bono translation in crisis situations or for charities. Some scholars have tried to come up with new terms to make more precise the definition of nonprofessional translation, such as the coinages "cyberdubbing" and "cybersubtitling" by Rocío Baños and Jorge Díaz-Cintas (2023), which focus on the online practices of subtitling and dubbing. The problems with this in relation to the fan translation context are that (1) it potentially includes any type of online subtitling or dubbing, no matter whether it is professional or nonprofessional, or what purpose it is created for, and (2) it only includes the modalities of subtitling and dubbing, whereas fan translation can cover many other practices.[2] Minako O'Hagan's (2009) term, "user-generated translation" suffers the same problems as it lumps together fan translation with other amateur forms of translation, all of which could be considered "free labor" (Terranova 2000) as they go unpaid but still contribute to the online economy.[3] Each of these terms shows that the discipline of translation studies was, and still is, struggling to deal with translation practices that do not fit within the existing conceptualization of translation, which typically takes professional translation as paradigmatic, where professional translation is understood as work commissioned by an editor or a translation agency and undertaken by someone who sees themselves as a translator. With the general move of translation, both professional and otherwise, online, the boundaries of professional translation practice are blurring as translations can be done by people who do not see themselves as translators, or are not commissioned to do translations, or it can be done by machine translation, such as Google Translate (among many others).[4] We thus prefer to use the term "fan translation" as this not only identifies who is doing the translation (fans!) but also positions it within the existing scholarship on fandom. Equally, it allows us to distinguish fan translation from other forms of amateur, unpaid, and nonprofessional translation work.[5]

Fansubbing

Fan translation can take place in any type of fandom, and so there could be fan translations of everything from popular media to board games, or even news or literary texts. The great majority of existing research has privileged fan audiovisual translation, especially fansubbing. One reason for this is the fact that there is a great deal of it out there and it has been relatively easy to find. Compared with many other forms of translation, subtitling requires relatively little technological knowledge to produce: fansubbers just need to find subtitling software and files to subtitle. There are many open-source subtitling programs, and files can be sourced (illegally) from torrent sites, or more recently, by downloading them from video-sharing sites. Other genres, especially video games, require much more technological skill and therefore have a higher barrier to entry.

One of the first scholarly mentions of fan translation appears in Abé Mark Nornes's article "For an Abusive Subtitling" (1999). Nornes rails against the conventional form of subtitling that he sees as "corrupt" as it hides or removes the elements of otherness from the media text being translated (Nornes 1999, 18). We could see this as removing—or at least attenuating—the "cultural odor" (Iwabuchi 2002, 27) of the source text, that is, the features that link it to a specific cultural origin and which, following Koichi Iwabuchi, are viewed positively by consumers. This complaint about translation also surfaces, in slightly different forms, in the work on literary translation by Lawrence Venuti (1995) and Emily Apter (2013); translation always risks removing the cultural specificness of texts, and this is especially the case with subtitles due to the various constraints (such as time on screen, number of characters per line, placement at the bottom of the screen, etc.) that are part of professional subtitling practice.[6] Nornes proposes in its place what he calls an "abusive" subtitling: one that makes the practice of translation visible in the subtitling through using nonstandard language and experimenting with language, or by the use of visual techniques such as different size fonts, different fonts, or different colored text. One of the examples of this "abusive" subtitling that Nornes offers is based on fan subtitles of *Ranma ½* and the ways in which the translators have used all these techniques in order to make it more readable within the fan community (Nornes 1999, 31–2).

It is telling that this first relatively well-known example comes from anime fan subtitling. Nornes is an expert in Japanese cinema and has subtitled from Japanese, so it should come as no surprise that he works on a Japanese context. At the same time, *Ranma ½* is mentioned by Sean Leonard (2005, 291) as one of the first widely distributed fansubbed videos, demonstrating how a lot of early fansubbing took place in the context of anime fandom. In the anecdote from Jenkins which began our book, he also mentions practices of watching untranslated anime, with interactive, real-time translation from the audience (Jenkins 1992, 76). Fansubbing in this community responded to an interest in Japanese cartoons that was not being served by official releases as Leonard (2005, 291) argues, or official releases being adapted significantly in translation (Ruh 2010), with a classic example being *Robotech*, which adapts *Macross* (Nornes 2007, 195). Distribution at this time was by tape, which made it harder than today when anyone can easily find dubbed or subtitled versions of *Ranma ½* on YouTube. This meant it tended to remain within the fan community and was connected to conventions or small mailing distributors. Nornes's attention to this fansub, then, sets up fansubbing as (1) oppositional to mainstream subtitling and (2) connected to the subculture of anime fans.[7] This has been influential on work that came after Nornes, with many scholars positioning the history of fansubbing in relation to anime (e.g., Ferrer Simó 2005; Díaz-Cintas and Muñoz Sánchez 2006; Pérez-González 2006, 2020; Dwyer 2012, 2018).

Fansubbing has since gone far beyond anime. In informal film distribution, it can be found in many contexts (Crisp 2015, 108–10). In the Italian context, Luca Barra (2009) and Serenella Massidda (2015) have explored the fansubbing of popular American TV shows such as *Lost* (2004–10). They both focus on the practices of fansubbers and how they organize their work, including sourcing texts, translating them, and revising the translations. Massidda goes further to analyze the strategies they use, which she argues lead to translations which resemble more closely the dialogue in English than in professional translations (Massidda 2015, 81–93). In relation to China, Dingkun Wang (2017) has examined the strategies used by fansubbers, while Kelly Hu (2013) and Weiyu Zhang and Chengting Mao (2013) consider more how fansubbing functions within the complex Chinese media ecosystem. Further work has considered Poland and the Czech Republic (Luczaj, Holy-Luczaj, and Cwiek-Rolgalska 2014), Sweden

(Pedersen 2019), and Thailand (Wongseree, O'Hagan, and Sasamoto 2019), and research can be found in other contexts.

Much of this scholarship focuses on what it is that fansubbers are doing in terms of their practices, either in the sense of how the group is organized or how they translate texts. While the national and linguistic contexts for this are different in each of the case studies, it is remarkable how consistent the findings tend to be in relation to translation strategies. While there are still some unconventional strategies (from the point of view of professional practice, which tends to rely on linguistically adaptive, single-color subtitles at the bottom of the screen [Díaz-Cintas and Remael 2021]), the translations tend not to be as wildly "abusive" as Nornes found. There may still be headnotes, which are like a footnote but at the top of the screen, or the translation may be more literal or follow the original text more closely than in professional practice, but there is much less linguistic or graphic experimentation than Nornes discussed. Jan Pedersen (2019) even concludes his study of fansubs in Sweden by noting that they are not very creative. The subcultural nature of fansubbing that was inherent in its identification with anime in the United States is also reduced by the fact that many of the shows being subtitled—*Lost* and *Californication* in Massidda's work, *The Big Bang Theory* in Wang's—are mainstream American TV shows that were very popular at the time they were being subtitled. Fansubbing in these cases is not responding to a lack of translations, as anime fansubbing was (Leonard 2005), but rather that conventional translations are not what audiences want or are not appearing fast enough. In some ways, then, fansubbing reinforces existing cultural flows, rather than challenging them.[8] It is also notable that much of this work was written before the growth of streaming TV (e.g., Netflix or Amazon Prime), which has significantly altered the availability of media texts and their translations (Choi, Kim, and Evans 2023): in such a context, it is now much easier to get hold of a great variety of texts and often both a dubbed and a subtitled version, which may render much fansubbing—which aimed to make previously untranslated texts available—somewhat redundant.

Fansubbing was being incorporated into some viewing platforms in the early 2010s. Tessa Dwyer (2012, 2017, 164–85) focuses on the way that Rakuten Viki, which distributes Japanese, Korean, Taiwanese, and Chinese films and TV shows, has used the energy of fansubbers by offering the opportunity to take part in the subtitling of these shows and films. Rakuten Viki differs from fansubbing as it has the license to distribute the shows, thus blurring the line between professional translation and fansubs (Dwyer 2017, 176). As Dwyer (2017, 172) also points out, Rakuten Viki has been instrumental in making available a significant amount of East Asian media content in the English-speaking world, though, again, this is also now happening on other streaming platforms like Netflix. Furthermore, Rakuten Viki has also worked to develop media accessibility and subtitles for smaller and endangered languages (Dwyer 2018, 444–5). It is not straightforwardly possible, then, to see Rakuten Viki's use of fansubbing as exploitational, even though it could be considered so in the sense of using freely given labor in a monetized environment. The commitment to community, accessibility, and showcasing media that might not usually get translated suggests something more complicated: a social commitment that has been adapted to survive in a commercial marketplace. The slipperiness of this and its conceptual fluidity highlights the continuing complexity of understanding free labor on the internet (Terranova 2000) and the interactions between users and distributors in co-creational labor (Banks and Deuze 2009): they are neither simply emancipatory nor exploitative but combine elements of these seemingly contradictory aspects.

Fansubbing can be more oppositional in intent, and some scholars have linked it to activism. This has especially been the case in China, which operates quite strict media and internet censorship. The sort of fan activism discussed by Zhang and Mao (2013), which focuses on making content available, which included some free-to-view training courses in what might be called civics education, or the rather diffuse sense of activism as something that seeks to evade government control of media, put forward by Dingkun Wang and Xiaochun Zhang (2017), is based on the indirect challenge to censorship. In fact, some fan activities have been more supportive of the state (Wang and Ge 2023) and some scholars have doubted whether fansubbing of media products poses any sort of threat to the state (Morozov 2011, 69). It seems to us that "activism" can be a problematic term in this quite general sense, especially as such practices might not be seen as activist in other national contexts. More obviously activist are the unpaid translations of activist materials that are created for the purposes of creating social change (e.g., Baker 2016). It is also clear that there are links between fan practices and some forms of activism, as organizations like the Harry Potter Alliance have demonstrated (Jenkins et al. 2016). The precise instances of what is being translated, by whom, and for what goals need to be taken into account for an understanding of translation as activism. For example, Ting Guo (2021) examines how recent Chinese queer feminist fansubbing of US feminist documentaries aims to open up a space of discussion in mainland China which differs in many ways from existing activist practices, though still aims for social impact. Understanding "activism" in relation to fansubbing requires a strong and clear understanding of what "activism" entails, which often is more than just social impact but rather political and social change.

Fansubbing, we can conclude, is the modality of fan translation that has received the most attention from scholars in both translation and media studies. One reason for this is its ubiquity and visibility—it's become very easy to find—but also that many scholars in these disciplines are working on film and media or audiovisual translation and so tend to pay more attention to work in their areas. Fansubbing also has, as we mentioned, a relatively low barrier to entry, with the availability of free subtitling software and the facility of finding video files on the internet. Few scholars connect fansubbing with other fan activities, even though there are some clear overlaps in the activities. Nor have scholars sufficiently dealt with the impacts of new technologies such as streaming or the shift toward a more platform-based experience of the internet (Terranova 2022) and how they affect fansubbing as an activity.

Fandubbing, Romhacking, Scanlation, and Other Modalities

This section gives an overview of research on modalities of fan translation that have been discussed less than fansubbing. Fandubbing is one such modality. Dubbing requires more technological know-how than subtitling, though it is possible with free or open-source video editing software and ubiquitous technologies such as mobile phones or inbuilt microphones, so it has become within reach of fans. Early work on fandubbing compares it to professional practice (Nord, Khoshaligheh, and Ameri 2015), especially in the Iranian context. In this context, there are practices of "fundubbing," which tend to be more parodic and which do not aim to give a fair representation of the original dialogue, "fandubbing," which is undertaken by fans and which aims to be representative, and also some professional dubs that are informally shared as they have not been officially released (Nord, Khoshaligheh, and Ameri 2015, 3). This study notes that fandubs are often literal (Nord, Khoshaligheh, and Ameri 2015, 8) and even characterizes the translations as "poor." Professional dubbing practices tend to be less literal, partially due to the constraints of lip-synching across languages (see Chaume 2012 for a detailed discussion).[9]

More recent work has focused on the relationship between fandubbing, parody, and language learning in the case of the dubbing of songs in translation into Spanish and Catalan of mainly Japanese anime-related materials (Zhang and Vazquez-Calvo 2022) or the possibilities for language learning in the Bronie (male fans of *My Little Pony*) community through fandubbing (Shafirova and Cassany 2019). While the case of the fandubbed songs is viewed by the authors as a form of creative translation practice and a space for informal language learning, Jacob Mertens (2023) is more critical toward the parodic abridgments of anime with fandubbing that he analyzes. In these cases, the fandubbing and abridgment can change the representation of female characters or can trivialize the anime by overlooking its actual narrative to focus on moments that can be ridiculed. While there is something dialogic in this, as it could be read, tentatively, as a critique of the sexism in the text or the convoluted narrative, as Mertens (2023) notes, it also shows a lack of respect for the original text. This is not a common feature of most fan translations that we have discussed so far, most of which aim for a representative form of translation, that is, one that shows what's in the text: Mertens's case studies, on the other hand, use the source text as a jumping-off point for jokes. The ethics of this is somewhat complicated: on the one hand, there is a freedom to interpret, but also there is the possibility of interpreting in a way that is against what the original creators would have wanted. This tension is not easily resolved and affects fan fiction more widely (Jenkins 1992, 152–222). It becomes more of a problem if the abridged and fandubbed form is the only one that viewers encounter, which gives them a distorted image of the original. Older parodic dubs, such as *What's Up, Tiger Lily?* (Woody Allen, 1966) or *La dialectique peut-elle casser des briques?/Can Dialectics Break Bricks?* (Réné Viénet, 1973; see Dwyer 2017, 79–96) never presented themselves as a fair representation of their source films and so would always be read as parodies, whereas abridgments on YouTube are harder to recognize as parodic or not representational.[10] Fandubs, like other translations, have significant potential to affect how viewers perceive texts.

Fan translations of video games have also been studied. They are understood to come about due to either fans considering that the official localization is low quality or because the game has not been localized into that language (O'Hagan and Mangiron 2013, 301–2). This translation process is sometimes called "romhacking" (Muñoz Sánchez 2009), as game software, especially on consoles, was known as ROMs.[11] Romhacking is harder to do than other forms of fan translation as it requires technical as well as linguistic skills (O'Hagan and Mangiron 2013, 300). The early work on fan localization (Muñoz Sánchez 2008, 2009; O'Hagan 2009, 102–10) tends to focus on comparing it with professional practice: romhacked translations are typically less adaptive than official translations. As fan translators of video games are less limited by forms of censorship, they can use taboo language, sexual content, or copyrighted brand names (Muñoz Sánchez 2009, 178). This can lead to a playing experience which is closer to the original language than official translations; fans typically prefer this closer version (O'Hagan and Mangiron 2013, 303). More recent work on romhacking has highlighted how it can be useful for language learning (Vazquez-Calvo 2021), especially in the framework of a small language like Catalan. One example where fan localization of video games has been studied in the context of gaming is Mia Consalvo's book, *From Atari to Zelda* (2016, especially pages 41–64). Consalvo analyzes fan translations in relation to English-speaking translators' deepening understanding of Japanese culture through video gaming: for her, fan translation can be an opening onto a more cosmopolitan outlook. Despite this, significantly more could be written about how romhacking fits in with other aspects of fan and gaming culture.

The fan translation of comics, known as scanlation, has received much more scholarly attention than romhacking. Following the usual pattern of work on fan translation, earlier work on the topic analyzes how fan practices differ from professional ones and how the development of computer technologies has facilitated it (Deppey 2005; Trykowska 2009). As with other fan translation practices, fans tend to be more literal translators than professionals and tend to translate works that are not otherwise available. As with fansubbing, there is considerable focus on the translation of Japanese comics (manga) into English and other languages (Fabbretti 2015; Madeley 2015; Moura Aragão 2016; Tremblay 2018), although, in theory, there is no reason why the numerous comics traditions from other nations and languages cannot be fan translated. There is some work on the fan translation of Boys' Love comics between Japanese and Chinese (Yang and Xu 2017) which positions it as a form of "globalization from below," that is, challenging the usual media flows and showing a grassroots cosmopolitanism, something that can be said of other transnational fan practices.

Translating songs is another area that has received some attention from scholars looking at fan translation practices. There is an enormous quantity of song translations available on the internet, often on lyrics forums. There is a little research in this area, with some on the strategies used by fan translators of Morrissey (Kaross and Spinola 2012) or on the way fan-created paratexts of K-pop songs help readers understand the cultural context (Cruz, Seo, and Binay 2021). More interestingly, Şebnem Susam-Saraeva (2015, 143–56) places fan translation in a wider historical and social context of Greek and Turkish relations, which affords more possibility for understanding it beyond ideas of accessing texts or language learning.

There is also some work on the fan translation of popular fiction, often focusing on Harry Potter translations that came about due to the official translation taking time (e.g., Chan 2010, 137–40; Evans 2020a, 179–80; Borodo 2022, 441–2). A more recent phenomenon has been the translation of Chinese-language web fiction (i.e., fiction first published on the internet) into English by fans, which has been discussed in relation to digital globalization (Wu 2021), that is, the increasingly global nature of the internet and increased interactions between cultures as a result. A prominent genre here is *wuxia* fiction, a genre of Chinese popular literature which depicts martial artists' adventures in ancient China (Li 2021; Chang and Zhao 2022), suggesting that fan translation can bring attention to previously less circulated forms, as we also saw in other media.

This section has highlighted how much of the work on fan translations beyond fansubbing has focused mainly on the strategies used by translators and how they differ from professional practice. This is obviously an important starting point, but does not address why the texts are translated, beyond giving access to them, or what sorts of interventions they might be making in a (fan) culture. A smaller number of works mention language learning, and this can be an important motivation for fan translators, as translation helps them learn their language skills (Lakarnchua 2017). This works best for prestigious languages like English or Japanese, which tend to be the main sources discussed in the articles. Only a handful of articles address more complex topics: parody and its relation to translation, or the ways in which fan translation might be embedded in a particular cultural dynamic (e.g., between Turkey and Greece). Surprisingly little research connects fan translations to transcultural fandom (Chin and Morimoto 2013) or other fan practices (such as cosplay or fanfic). Reflecting on these lesser-explored topics would open some very new paths in fan translation scholarship and deepen understanding of the phenomenon. We aim to do this in Chapters 3 and 4 of this book.

The Specter of Copyright

One area we have not mentioned yet, but which both deserves discussion and has been researched by many scholars, is the issue of copyright. Copyright laws differ from jurisdiction to jurisdiction—for example, British copyright law, in the form of the Copyrights, Designs and Patents Act 1988, differs from the United States' copyright law in Title 17 of the US Code.[12] However, to reach some sort of international consensus on copyright, there is an underlying treaty that many countries have signed up to and which is the basis for their copyright law: the Berne Convention.[13] The Berne Convention was originally written in the late 1880s and has been revised regularly since then, with the last major revision taking place in 1971 in Paris, with further amendments in 1979. This is before many digital types of publishing and even certain genres of work, though the provisions cover most of what we would think of as digital objects as "literary and artistic works" (Article 2, §1), and the text explicitly mentions cinematographic works (i.e., film). Importantly for the discussion of fan translation, the Berne Convention specifically mentions translations and associated rights in Article 8, which states:

> Authors of literary and artistic works protected by this Convention shall enjoy the exclusive right of making and of authorizing the translation of their works throughout the term of protection of their rights in the original works.

In other words, translations made without the permission of copyright holders during the term of copyright would be an infringement of copyright if the country follows the Berne Convention. Translations are understood as "derivative works" in US law (17 USCode §101) and "adaptations" in British law (Copyrights, Designs and Patents Act 1998, Section 21(3)(a)(i)), and are restricted practices that need permission. This means that, in many cases, fan translations are copyright infringing, as they do not have the relevant permissions in order to produce translations.[14]

There are some provisions for exceptions to the restrictions of copyright law, under what is known as "Fair Practice" in the Berne Convention (Article 10), "Fair Use" in American law (17 USCode §107), and "Fair Dealing" in British law (Copyrights, Designs and Patents Act 1998, Sections 28–76). These exceptions typically include copying for research or personal use as well as criticism and news reporting, but they often relate to using a limited quantity of the work and seldom allow commercial purposes. The precise wording of what is allowed is different in each law, and the precise quantity is seldom specified, which makes it difficult to define precisely what is Fair Practice in each jurisdiction. In theory (following the laws we've mentioned), a translation of a short passage of a text used in a critical work would be a form of Fair Practice, as would a short translation produced for personal use. Again, much fan translation goes beyond the translation of short passages, even if there is no intent to commercially exploit (i.e., sell or otherwise monetize) the translation, and so would be an infringement of copyright.

Two judgments, both from 2017, have clarified the position of fan translation in European law. The first was in the Netherlands, where the group Free Subtitles Foundation took the anti-piracy organization BREIN to court over whether or not subtitles could be created and distributed. The court ruled that subtitles were covered by copyright and so needed permission from the copyright holder (Anthony 2017). The second took place in Sweden, where the operator of the site undertexter .se was fined 217,000 kronor (*c.* US$27,000 or £20,000 at the time) for copyright infringement over the placing of (fan-made) film subtitles online (Van der Sar 2017). The defense argued that the subtitles were additional to the film, rather than an integral part of it, though this did not convince the court (Van der Sar 2017). What is interesting about this case is that it was not the subtitlers themselves that were prosecuted, but rather the founder of the site that aggregated them. This pattern was also followed in 2021 when Chinese authorities prosecuted the fansubbing group YYeTs over piracy, though in that case, there was also more clear financial exploitation of the fansubs through fees for members and advertisers (Xinhua 2021). As such, it seems that the motive for prosecution is not so much for producing subtitles but for distributing them, possibly attached to unauthorized versions of the films and TV shows they translate. We are not aware of any prosecutions in other forms of fan translation, but this might be because copyright owners have issued Cease and Desist letters (or their local equivalent), which have led to the materials being removed from the internet without much fanfare.

While these cases demonstrate and set precedents for the copyright status of fansubbing and fan translation more generally, the new European Digital Services Act,[15] which became applicable in February 2024, requires platforms and hosting services to take down "illegal content." This term is vague but could refer to hate speech, illegal services, or, possibly, material that infringes copyright. Many international platforms have been making changes to their interfaces since August 2023 to make it easier to report such illegal content. It is unclear, at the time of writing, what effect this will have on fan translation in the EU, though we expect it will reduce it significantly.

The legal situation of fan translation has been written about extensively in fan studies, mainly in relation to Japanese comics and cartoons (Hatcher 2005; Lee 2009; Lee 2011; Denison 2011; Tremblay 2018; Zhu 2023). Earlier work on the relationship between fan translation and copyright tended to focus on the ways in which fan translators would focus on texts that were not available in the target language, rather than trying to compete with official translations (e.g., Lee 2009, 1016–17). Whether fan translators actually follow these codes of ethics has been brought into doubt by later work (e.g., Denison 2011, 459–61). In the beginning, anime distributors tended toward a hands-off approach, but this had changed by the time Rayna Denison was writing in 2011, with distributors like FUNimation sending Cease and Desist letters to fansubbing groups (Denison 2011, 462). The changing field of distribution has also affected relationships between the industry and fansubbers (Tremblay 2018), though as yet little has been written about how streaming platforms, such as Netflix or Crunchyroll and their large libraries of content, have affected fan translators.

As most of the existing work is on copyright and fan translation of anime, it overlooks the issues faced in other areas, such as the Italian practices discussed earlier, where mainstream American dramas were translated faster and in a different format (subtitled rather than dubbed) than official broadcast translations. It was this "hunger for source content," not yet available officially, which Alyssa Tremblay sees as defining fan translation as distinct from other fan practices, which focus more on remediation and creative critique (Tremblay 2018, 328). We would argue that translation is a creative and critical act, although it is, in most cases, more restricted by the original text than fan fiction or similar practices. Taking a less instrumental approach to translation—understanding it more as an interpretative activity that shows creativity—wouldn't change the legal status of it,[16] but would help to understand why people are led to undertake their own translations. If they just wanted source content, then learning the language would be enough: translating is an activity in itself.

The legal status of fan translation may, in some ways, have limited the research on it. Not only does it necessitate going through ethical approval from institutions to write about fan translation, but also caution about discussing or identifying participants.[17] Furthermore, it may lead participants to be reticent about taking part in any research, though, in our experience, many fan translation groups are willing to work with researchers.

Where Next?

While the work on fan translation in general has been developing and has started to offer nuanced reflections on the practice, there are ways in which it can develop further. Moving beyond comparisons with professional practice or questions of legality, which have been central to much of the existing work, seems an obvious step, as would considering the changing position of fan translation following the growth of streaming platforms, as we have already mentioned. We would also like to suggest two further ways of developing the discussion: considering translation as a craft and exploring fragmentary translations, rather than just whole texts.[18]

The idea that translation is a craft is not new: there's an anthology of writings on translation by translators called *The Craft of Translation* from 1989 (Biguenet and Schulte 1989).

Craft has been recently rethought by scholars such as Richard Sennett (2008) and David Gauntlett (2018). Both of them try to move the understanding of craft away from considering it as something pre-industrial to include different forms of production, including digital ones (Gauntlett 2018, 91–111). For Sennett, craft is "good work that is done for its own sake" (2008, 20). That is, craft is concerned with producing something that is of high quality for its own intrinsic rewards, such as pleasure or satisfaction, as opposed to churning out poor-quality products. There is no reason why craft can't be profitable, though there are societal pressures that affect the profitability of working to a high standard. Craft, for Sennett, can be physical work—the traditional view of it being making objects through some form of handiwork—or more intellectual work such as musicianship or writing. To us, it seems obvious that translation can be understood as a craft in these terms: it can be done to a high standard for its own sake, and one would assume that a translator would want to reach high standards of quality. We see no reason why this could not also apply to fan translators, who are often self-motivated and want to reach high standards, even if those standards are different from professional translation (Nornes 1999; Schules 2014). Sennett also argues that "thinking and feeling are contained within the process of making" (2008, 7), that is, crafting is a way of interacting with the world and oneself that includes modes of thought and affect. One can think through making. Understanding (fan) translation as a craft makes it into a meaningful activity of making in itself, and this changes how it is approached: not just as a means to an end (e.g., distributing media from other languages) but also as an end in itself. This means that the products of (fan) translation are worthy of scrutiny and consideration for how they embody the thinking and feeling of their creators.

Translators writing about translation, as in *The Craft of Translation* or other volumes like *The Translator as Writer* (Bassnett and Bush 2006), Clive Scott's *Translating Baudelaire* (2000), or, in a less academic style, Kate Briggs's translation memoir *This Little Art* (2017), often reflect on the process of translation and the rewards that it brings, as well as assuming that translations themselves are worthy objects of close study. Yet fan translation work seldom hears the voice of fan translators themselves (possibly, as we have said, due to the illegality of the activity and risks associated with that). Thinking of translating as a craft activity also allows readers to become more aware of the transformative processes involved in translating.

It is not just the intrinsic creativity of translation that becomes clearer when thinking of it as a craft, but also its social nature. David Gauntlett (2018, 10) argues that making things is a social activity, that is, we make things to join communities of makers or to connect with other people through sharing or selling those things. This can take place on the internet or in person, or in some combination of the two. This takes us back to Jenkins's reflections on fan cultures as communities and the connection between fan production and the fan community, which is also the case for fan translations. Exploring translation as a social act, and how it generates or maintains networks of people, would develop an understanding of fan translation as a social activity beyond questions of labor and media distribution. We explore this in Chapter 4 when we discuss queer fan translations. "Craft" therefore seems to us a useful concept for deepening the understanding of fan translation, and translation in general, as a form of socially embedded making.

A second area for development is thinking about the translation of fragments in other texts or in short forms. Cultural products spread and travel not only as full texts but in shortened forms such as clips or as quotes in other texts (Jenkins, Ford, and Green 2013). This can take place both in born-digital texts, such as blogs, microblogging, video reviews, and so on, but also in analogue forms, such as in fanzines. Quotations can also cross sign systems, from speech to writing, or the other way around. Almost all existing work on fan translation focuses on full texts—films, TV shows, video games, songs—but what if the attention moved to looking at how other forms of fan production also used translation? How does fan discourse about TV in a foreign language engage with that language? How does fan criticism discuss international movies and cite from them? Moving away from full texts allows a wider and more generalized consideration of fan translation and reveals that many people are translating, even if they might not consider themselves translators. Researching more fragmentary translations might mean combing fanzines and blogs for discussions of texts that use translation, or examining review videos for how they have translated (or not) citations from the media under discussion. (As we do in Chapter 3 in our discussion of board game videos.) In fields where *danmaku* (comments on screen) are used, these *danmaku* are sometimes translational and show how fans are reading interlingually (Yang 2020; see also Chapter 5 of this book). Another approach is to examine what Dingkun Wang (2022) has called "translational remixes," that is, remix or fan vids that also include translation of the source materials. Translating is thus embedded in another form of fan practice, rather than separate or parallel to it. This approach makes translation more clearly into a fan practice that operates with and through other practices.

These two suggestions, then, bring attention back to the process of making and its transformative nature in translation, as well as the social nature of that making, and open up new avenues of research in terms of shorter forms that might be embedded in other fan practices. They thus go beyond existing scholarship and open new paths that help to cement the position of translation as a practice in studies of fandom.

CHAPTER THREE

Beyond the Global North

On Disney+, there's a show called *L-Pop*.[1] The show was produced in 2023 and tells the story of a K-pop fan, Andrea (Andrea de Alba), as she tries to put together a K-pop dance team in Mexico City. Andrea is a bit disorganized and not always the greatest dancer, but she tries her best. What drew us to this show was that it was a Spanish-language show on Disney+, not something that we were expecting to find in the UK where we have our subscription. It was a fun, family-friendly watch, but the reason we speak of it here is that it is one of the few representations of fandom on TV that we have seen from Mexico or Latin America more generally.[2] Access to media in languages other than English has improved in the UK in recent years, but on a predominantly English-language platform like Disney+, we did not expect to find much material originally in another language. *L-Pop*'s focus on fans in Mexico made us think about one of the wider issues in fan studies: how English-language-focused it is.

At conferences, we've heard fan studies scholars whose first language wasn't English talk about how the language of fandom is English. This is reflected in the scholarship: for example, in *Seeing Fans* (Bennett and Booth 2016), of the twenty-five chapters, only three are clearly about fans outside of English-speaking contexts (Hampton 2016; Lamerichs 2016; Morimoto 2016).[3] In *Fandom: Identities and Communities in a Mediated World* (Gray, Sandvoss, and Harrington 2007), there is a section on "Fan Audiences Worldwide," which includes work on Indian film fans (Punathambekar 2007), East Asian cinema fans (Chin 2007) and film fandom in South Korea (Ciecko and Lee 2007). The whole section is four of the twenty-six chapters in the book and is very focused on film. *The Routledge Companion to Media Fandom* (Click and Scott 2018) has a section on "Race and Transcultural Fandom" which consists of seven chapters, from the volume's forty-four. One of those chapters (Warner 2018) focuses on Black female fans in the United States, so is English-language focused, even if its focus on Black women, race, and fandom is entirely necessary, given the historical lack of focus on race in fan studies (Wanzo 2015; Pande 2018; Woo 2018; TWC Editor 2023). This is not to say there is no work on fans working outside of English (examples include, among others, Kelly 2004 on Japanese fans; Chaturvedi, Singh, and Singh 2021 on Indian fans; Chen and Lam 2023 on Chinese fandoms), but that non-English fandoms are often seen as a smaller, distinct category that is marked by race or transculturality, rather than central to fan studies. Being a speaker of a specific language is distinct from, but sometimes overlaps with, other aspects of identity. This is especially the case for speakers of minoritized languages, such as Welsh in the UK (Coupland 2009).[4] As such, language can be an important element of how fandoms intersect with identities and communities which should be studied alongside other aspects of identity and their intersections. This chapter focuses on fan translation in the Global South and into languages other than English as a way of confronting the English-language bias of much fan studies work.

In fact, it's not just English-language fandoms that tend to be highlighted as the focus of fan studies work, but also, explicitly North American ones: Paul Booth and Lucy Bennett (2016, 8) note that "only very recently has scholarship acknowledged that the [fan] community has significant demographic representation of fans from racial and ethnic backgrounds other than white and middle-class *Americans*" (our emphasis). The fact that the special issue of *Transformative Works and*

Cultures on "European" fans (Kustritz 2015) includes English and Welsh fans, as well as Polish and Italian, suggests that even English-language speaking fans from outside North America are given a marked status in fan studies research, despite a number of fan studies scholars residing in the UK. Reading Benjamin Woo's thoughtful and nuanced discussion of whiteness in fan studies, one might be forgiven for thinking fandom only takes place in North America. The only country mentioned by name is the United States (Woo 2018, 246) and his discussion of fan conventions mentions two cities: Detroit (United States) and Toronto (Canada). Woo is explicitly anti-racist in this piece, but at the same time, the geographical locations of his discussion are severely limited, especially when discussing fan studies, which is internationally produced. Of course, the location of some fan studies scholars in North America may privilege North American fans as groups to study for those scholars, but when thinking about fandom more widely, it seems an oversight not to engage with the rest of the world. There is a risk of universalizing from what is actually a local position, as has been critiqued by decolonial scholars such as Walter D. Mignolo (2012) in other contexts: a truly global understanding of fandom would need to explore practices around the world and how they might differ or overlap.

Other chapters in *The Routledge Companion to Media Fandom* are more explicit about some of the issues researchers face when studying fans in other locations and languages. In discussion with Aswin Punathambekar and Sangita Shresthova, Bertha Chin cites not speaking the same language as being a problem for talking to and researching fans in other cultures. She recounts trying to research *Arrow* fans in China but could not get them to open up beyond simple communications as she did not speak Chinese (Chin, Punathambekar, and Shresthova 2018, 299). This is indeed a major hurdle, though arguably one that could be overcome by collaborating with someone who could speak Chinese. Methodologically, it is accepted that interviews work best when conducted in the participant's strongest language, as they are most likely to be comfortable speaking in that language and so give the most spontaneous answers. Another issue highlighted by Punathambekar in the same discussion (Chin, Punathambekar, and Shresthova 2018, 299) is the fact that scholars in fan and media studies seldom cite material created in "non-Western" contexts. One of the reasons for this is not being able to read it if it's in another language.[5] The result is that English becomes the default language of fan studies, and work in other languages is not read outside of them. A similar point was made about queer studies around twenty years ago: "Scholars writing in other languages and from other political and cultural perspectives read but are not, in turn, read" (Eng, Halberstam, and Muñoz 2005, 15). One solution to this problem is to take a position of "epistemological humility" (Eng, Halberstam, and Muñoz 2005, 15), that is, acknowledging these imbalances and seeking to right them, while also acknowledging that one's own positioning is not the only position that can be or is taken. Calls for de-Westernizing media studies have existed for longer still (Shohat and Stam 1994; Curran and Park 2000): focusing on practices in languages other than English would be one step in this direction.

You might expect translation studies, which is globally produced and read, to have addressed these imbalances more clearly. To an extent, it has: research is produced in many locations and about many language pairs, though there is still a predominance of English-language publishing, which is common across academia (e.g., Arenas-Castro et al. 2024). That said, there are journals publishing in other languages, and translation studies scholars are typically capable of reading at least two languages. The field has also reflected on its own Eurocentrism (van Doorslaer and Flynn 2013), especially the way in which it has created its own "mythistory" of a European origin (Baer 2020). Translation scholars have also considered the ways in which translation can alter and erase local traditions and ways of knowing (Bennett 2007). While there is still significant room for improvement in the field of translation studies,[6] there has been some reckoning with its perceived European roots and the complex historical baggage that comes with them. Being aware of the global practices and contexts for translation helps to get a more holistic sense of what translation is and how it affects people.

Attention to situations and practices outside the Global North and—importantly—to voices emanating from the Global South, which are often not in English, can thus offer new ways of theorizing. Working in a more literary context, Shu-mei Shih and Françoise Lionnet (2011) stress the entanglements of theorizing from outside of Europe and of European (primarily French) theories and their international versions. They propose the "creolization" of theory as one way to understand this. Their aim is a decolonial one, that is, it aims to undo colonial thinking and to highlight the existing ways of knowing in colonial locations, rather than proposing a form of knowledge-colonialism that would just take ideas from the Global South as fodder for new thinking in the North. Shih and Lionnet's focus on creolization offers an understanding that cultures are constantly in contact with one another and changing each other (2011, 24). Recognizing this offers a way to understand the globalized world we live in, where cultures are seldom unaffected by or unconnected to other ones. Yet, as we noted earlier, cultures are seldom seen as equal: there are more hegemonic or powerful ones and others that are less so.[7] Therefore it is important to recognize that "the [existing] structures of knowledge are complicit with the structures of global inequality" (Shih and Lionnet 2011, 32). Shih and Lionnet's suggestion is to push for creolization of that knowledge as a way of reversing some of that inequality. Our focus on fan translation in the Global South, as well as our argument for understanding fandoms in the global context, is undertaken in this spirit. We want to understand how fandoms work in a globalized world, where national identities entangle with globalized ones (such as being a K-pop fan in Mexico, as in *L-Pop*). Translation is where the global and local come into contact.

Research on Fan Translation in the Global South

One way to develop the understanding of fan translation in the Global South is to see what is published on fan translation in the Global South. However, we found there were limitations to this when we tried. To get a sense of what was out there, we searched in three regionally influential journals in the field of translation studies: *Mutatis Mutandis* (published mainly in Spanish in Colombia), *Cadernos de Traduçao* (published mainly in Portuguese in Brazil), and the *Journal for Translation Studies in Africa* (published mainly in English in South Africa) for work on fan translation.[8] One of the difficulties of this was what word to use for "fan" as it is sometimes left in English and sometimes translated. The term in Spanish is *aficionado/a* and the term in Portuguese is *fã* or *amador/a*,[9] and we used these terms as well as "fan" in our searches. We found nothing in the *Journal for Translation Studies in Africa* on fan translation at all, although there was a special issue on "community translation" (Chachu and Liebze 2023), which shows there is an interest in nonprofessional forms of translation in African contexts, but not necessarily in relation to media fandom. *Mutatis Mutandis* similarly showed only a very small number of works about fan translation: one, in English, was about fan translation in Iran (Ameri and Khoshsaligheh 2019), and another was not really about fan translations as such but translations in the library of the Cuban author José Lezama Lima (Ramírez 2017), which was written by someone based at the University of California. Both these examples illustrate the complex ways national and international contexts are entangled across languages and cultures, as suggested by Shih and Lionnet's creolization of knowledge. In *Cadernos de Traduçao*, we found one article which was the Portuguese translation of an article originally published in English (Díaz-Cintas, Muñoz Sánchez, and Moura 2022). This sort of translation shows the circulation of knowledge, but from

North to South—there is far less translation in the other direction. Another article (Mundim 2001) dealt with fanfic as a form of intersemiotic translation (as discussed in Chapter 1). The third article that we found (Pappen 2023) investigated the role of translators in amateur theater—*amador* in Portuguese meaning both amateur and fan—and therefore had something to say about translation in a nonprofessional context but did not view the translator themselves as a fan or amateur. Beyond these journals, we also searched in the Mexican database Redalyc, which covers publications in Latin America, for "fan translation," "traducción aficionado," and "traduçao amador" and found the same results, with a handful (16) more for "fansub."[10] Searching "fan," on the other hand, led to 14,111 results, and "translation" led to 17,749.[11] There is therefore work around fans and translation, but not so much on fan translation. One reason for this might well be what Chin and Shresthova refer to as "institutional resistance" in their discussion of transcultural fandom (Chin, Punathambekar, and Shresthova 2018, 301). That is, the relative lack of funding or institutional recognition for working in this area, which would limit enthusiasm for it. However, there may be other reasons that are not so obviously apparent. There are clearly fans in Latin America—*L-Pop* shows that, as well as the findings on Redalyc—but how they interact with media in other languages seems to be under-researched.

There is research on fan translation practices in other locations in the Global South, though the number of studies is still quite low. It's important to remember that when we say the Global South, this actually means a rather heterogenous group of locations which all have different characteristics, rather than a single, homogeneous location. The same can be said of the Global North: the United States is different in many ways—legal, ideological, historical, economical, geographical—to the UK, for instance, and this has an effect on how fan cultures act and develop. As Chin notes, we should not assume that fan practices are the same the world over: her example is the difference between Australia and the United

States (Chin, Punathambekar, and Shresthova 2018, 300). To understand fan cultures, it is important to understand the wider national context they are in, which can mean everything from what magazines are regularly published to censorship, as well as whether there are stores selling physical products or a good library system. How does film fandom, also known as cinephilia, develop in places where cinema-going is difficult or prohibitively expensive? In order to understand fandoms, then, it is worth exploring the characteristics of the locale where they are found, and how they interact with and influence fandom formation. On a disciplinary level, that means drawing from area studies when doing fan studies. On a practical level, it means not taking for granted assumptions about what fandom is or how it is practiced, especially in locations that have been less studied. It also means not assuming that Africa, India, and South-East Asia, for instance, are the same: there are long and complex histories of each of those areas and their interactions with the rest of the world.[12] The level of nuance should not just be at the level of region or nation but also take into account the fact that there are different socioeconomic groups in a location that have different levels of resources and free time to put into fandom. Admittedly, this level of nuance is not always possible in a journal article with quite strict word limits, but this approach helps to avoid the issues of exclusion and assuming a single identity for fans which were criticized earlier in the chapter.

One example of this attention to local specificity in the scholarship is in a study of fansubbing in the Vietnamese context (Luong and Evans 2021). In addition to reviewing scholarship in English on translation in Vietnam more generally, Van Nhan Luong and Jonathan Evans (2021, 166–9) explore the economic and historical aspects of Vietnam in detail before discussing the history of translation in Vietnamese, in order to give context to their discussion of fan translations on YouTube. In the case of Vietnam, they argue, it is impossible to ignore the history of colonization as well as government censorship and internet penetration. Fan translation is thriving in Vietnamese, partially as a result of Vietnamese openness to translating texts, as well as the lack of availability of official translations. While some of the material translated came from English, many of the videos that Luong and Evans (2021, 171–3) found came from Korean and Chinese, suggesting the influence of K-pop and *hallyu* (the Korean wave) more generally, as well as Inter-Asian fandom. Much of what they found was also from TV shows and music videos, rather than films. They suggest reasons for this might include algorithms for removing proprietary content on YouTube, as well as the possibility of finding films elsewhere. While the article has its limits—it does not interview fans or use ethnographic methods, for instance—it does demonstrate the ways in which fan translation needs to be understood in relation to its wider national and international context. It also highlights the need to decenter English as the privileged language of fan studies, especially in contexts where English is not spoken. What it also demonstrates, though Luong and Evans do not mention this, is a sort of "minor transnationalism" (Lionnet and Shih 2005), where two less powerful cultures, such as Vietnamese and South Korean, interact without the mediation of a more powerful one (English). Minor transnationalisms can help to give a more nuanced and polycentric view of global culture and fandom's place within it.

In other studies, the practices of fansubbing are less clearly tied to their location. In a discussion of Thai fansubbing, for instance, Thandao Wongseree, Minako O'Hagan, and Ryoko Sasamoto (2019) position their study in relation to global discussions of fansubbing, which, as we saw in Chapter 2, tends to take American anime fansubbing as paradigmatic. While this helps to position the work in relation to studies of fan practices, it makes American practices hegemonic by making them unmarked. The article offers a new perspective on how trust functions in Thai fansubbing communities, with fans and nonfans having a different perspective (Wongseree, O'Hagan, and Sasamoto 2019, 6–7). The authors argue that fans are typically more trusting of fansubbing due to being part of the same fan community. It's not clear how generalizable this is, given that they looked at fans and fan translations of one specific reality TV show, *Leonningmaen/Running Man* (2011–current) from South Korea. It is hard to know if fans of other shows act in the same way, given the data presented in the article, though the idea that fans generally are more likely to trust fan productions seems reasonable. The authors do say that they conducted their empirical research in Thai (p. 3), but the citations from interviews and surveys have all been translated into English for publication. This was probably a recommendation of the journal where the article was published, but it erases the Thai language from the discussion and assumes a neutrality and transparency to translation that is methodologically questionable, given the interpretative nature of translation (see Chapter 1).

The existing cultural practices that fansubbing is embedded in are also important. In relation to Iran, for example, Saeed Ameri and Masood Khoshaligheh (2019, 436–7) discuss the introduction of subtitling and video piracy in Iran as well as censorship as the background to fansubbing in Persian (the language of Iran). They also compare fansubbing practices to professional practices, especially in relation to how taboo language is translated (2019, 438), though they also note that there is not really a subtitling tradition in Iran, where dubbing is more common in official translations (2019, 449). The corpus that they look at includes popular American films from the 1990s to the 2010s, but these may not be easily acceptable to Iranian censorship. They note that "Iranian authorities have tried hard to crack down on these [pirate] websites due to their unlicensed activities and the content that they share, which is deemed indecent and immoral according to Iranian culture" (2019, 442). It is not clear what, precisely, is being referred to here, but the difference in cultural acceptance will affect what films are officially translated and distributed, as well as what is chosen for fansubbing. Despite this atmosphere, what Saeed and Khoshaligheh found was that many fansubbers in Iran did so because they wanted to develop their English-language skills (as we saw in other cases in Chapter 2) and to have fun, as well as giving access to media content for other viewers (2019, 441). Some of this can be seen in their decisions to include explanatory material in the subtitles (2019, 446), which makes sense if you want to increase access and understanding of a text. Interviewees did not seem to mention censorship or any activist goals (in comparison to, e.g., the fansubbers discussed by Guo 2021), which may well be the case if they are just approaching it for language learning, though there are other ways of learning a language or accessing primary sources—not all language learners get involved in fansubbing. What is more likely is there is an interest in the world outside of Iran, which can be accessed, at least partially, in fansubbed material.

These three examples show that, while there is some similarity in practices of fan translation in the Global South, they are affected by local factors, including history, censorship, translation traditions, and access to texts. Just focusing on practices is not enough to explain how these differ from place to place. Yet they also open up understandings of how media travel and how the global media system is viewed by people outside of the Global North and its centers of media production. What we see is a more polycentric world, where Hollywood is provincialized. There is obviously more to do in finding out about translation in other media (e.g., songs, see, e.g., Susam-Saraeva 2015) and how that reflects or contradicts existing understandings, which would lead to a fuller, more globally oriented fan and media studies.

Board Game Fan Translation in Mexico

In this section, we use a short example to demonstrate ways of examining two areas that are underrepresented in fan translation research, board gamers and Mexico. By board gamers, we mean people who regularly play modern board games such as *Catan* (1995), *Carcassonne* (2002), or

Terraforming Mars (2016).[13] As Paul Booth (2018) has argued, board gamers are typically not studied in relation to fandom, partially as board games are seldom studied in media studies. This might be changing—Booth's own *Board Games as Media* (2021) demonstrates ways in which games can be studied using media and fan studies frameworks—but it is true that much fan studies work remains linked to screen media, as the focus on fansubbing in the previous section also demonstrated. We agree with Booth that board gamers are fans, especially when you take into account the vast amount of board game discourse on the internet, ranging from review websites to live play videos on YouTube, and the mega-forum that is Board Game Geek (a top 1,000 website in the United States, according to Booth 2021, 111). Board gamers discuss new games, trade tips on how to play, explain rules to each other, criticize game publishers' decisions, create game variants, and so on. They are thus productive fans as well as being emotionally connected to the games they play. Board games have not received much attention from translation studies (with exceptions including Evans 2013, 2020b), perhaps because they are not as prestigious a form of media as literature or film, even though board gaming is international and typically relies on translation due to the fact that games are produced globally in different languages (Evans 2020b).

Gaming culture is not the same the world over. For example, Cantonese and Mandarin speakers in Hong Kong tend to play games more socially, that is, as a way of interacting in groups and making friends, rather than the more hobby-oriented playing of the English speakers in the same city (Harrington 2023). This is seen in the games chosen by the two groups Jonathan Harrington studied: the predominantly Cantonese-language play groups preferred games of social deduction like *Werewolf* (1986), while the English-language groups preferred more Euro-style games that had heavier rules, such as *Terraforming Mars* (Harrington 2023).[14] The English-speaking group also had more focus on novelty, rather than ease of playing (Harrington 2023). Harrington argues that one reason for this is lack of access to the games, as many were published in English, and so the Cantonese-speaking players would have to work outside of the group's playing language. This did not mean they did not play them, but rather they played less of them. We assume there would be some translation at the table, as well, in order to include players whose English was not as confident, but Harrington did not report on this. The issue of language and unequal distribution of game materials is not limited to Hong Kong. As Enrique Uribe-Jongbloed (2020) recounts, he had to play *Dungeons and Dragons* in English in Colombia when he was younger, working with his own translations and translanguaging (changing language) at the table where necessary. This was a common experience at the time and meant that playing *Dungeons and Dragons* required a certain amount of English-language skill and other players who would also be able to shift between languages. This is a sort of fan translation that is difficult to document as it is ephemeral and takes place only when playing. While Uribe-Jongbloed describes it in relation to role-playing games in Colombia, we have argued elsewhere that it is a common feature of game playing (Evans 2020b).

Beyond these difficult to document moments of translation during play, there are also translations used in the discourse on board games. Our examples of this come from Mexican board game videos on YouTube. Translation here is fragmentary, that is, in parts, rather than of the whole text: it is embedded in the review rather than a replacement for the rule set. While Mexico is not a typical focus of fan studies scholarship, there has been some work on K-pop in Mexico as part of Latin America more generally (Madrid-Morales and Lovric 2015; Han 2017; Min, Jin, and Han 2019; Amaral et al. 2024). There is little research on boardgaming in Mexico. As a member of the North American Free Trade Agreement (NAFTA), Mexico has a free trade agreement with the United States, which means that American-produced board games are distributed in Mexico. This will affect what games are available, which in turn affects the gaming culture. This is reflected in the games we see in the videos, many of which come from North America or are North American versions of games from elsewhere.

We searched the term "reseñas de juegos de mesa Mexico" (board game reviews Mexico)[15] on YouTube and filtered by the location of the channel to find Mexican channels. Here we focus on one, Boardies Games, run by Rob Campos, in order to understand how the channel uses translation within reviews and how to play videos for games in English. The channel is in Spanish, with automatically produced subtitles in Spanish. Human-generated subtitles, which are typically better paced and more accurate, would be more accessibility-friendly, though obviously also more expensive to produce as a person needs to be paid to produce them, while automated subtitles are effectively free to use. On its homepage,[16] Boardies Games provides lists for different categories of videos: Juegos de mesa mexicanos (Mexican board games), Juegos de fiesta (party games), Top 10, Juegos de estrategia (strategy games), Juegos rápidos (quick games, though the channel translates this as "fillers"). These categories are similar to, if less detailed than, the ones used on Board Game Geek and in the English-language discourse on games, with the exception of "Mexican board games": this category appeals to an audience in Mexico who want to play locally produced games, as well as the wider Spanish-speaking audience who want to play games in Spanish.[17] The fact that the other categories closely mirror those used in English-language board gaming discourse suggests the influence of English terms and American gaming culture. The way the channel offers "filler" as a translation of *juegos rápidos* also echoes the English-language terminology, where this is a common term for a game with a quick playtime that can be used to fill in while other games are being set up. As such, it seems that the gaming culture in these videos, while mainly in Spanish, is linked to the English language through translation as well as through the actual availability of games.

To understand better how translation functions in these videos, we turn to a specific example. The video "Exploding Kittens: Cómo Jugar + Reseña" (Exploding Kittens: how to play + review)[18] explains how to play the English-language game *Exploding Kittens* (2015) in Spanish. The cards in the game have some text on them to explain their powers, and it's likely you would need some familiarity with English to play the game, as the symbols on the cards do not tell you the specific powers of the card. The title of the game is not translated in the video, but it is explained: "Si a ti, te gustan los gatos, las explosiones, y los gatos que explotan, este juego es para ti" (If you like cats, explosions, and cats that explode, this game is for you). The use of the *tú* form of address, which is less formal and more familiar, makes the connection between the viewer and the presenter seem friendly (rather than using a more formal *usted*). Discussing how to set up the game, Campos says "retiramos las seis tarjetas de *defuse*" (take away the six Defuse cards), not translating the name of the card when he says it. The term in Spanish would be something like *desactivar*, which sounds quite different to "defuse." Players watching need some English to follow this explanation, though as the card is shown, it is possible that they could see which one is meant. This strategy is not used consistently: for the next card, which is called "Exploding Kitten" in English, Campos uses the term "tarjeta de bomba" (bomb card), which explains the function of the card very well while dropping the title. Defuse is later explained as the only cards that can save you from the bomb: here the term is still not translated by a single word but it is explained clearly. The Exploding Kitten cards are later referred to as "gatitos explosivos" (explosive kittens). Some other cards are translated into Spanish, with their English versions displayed on screen, for example, "Ver el futuro" (See the Future), with others using both languages, for example, "Skip o saltar" (Skip or [skip in Spanish]) or just the English, for example, "Nope." The inconsistency of this strategy goes against the typical norms of translation, where almost everything would need to be translated (as it typically is in game translations; Evans 2013). Here it allows the viewer to both understand what is happening by explaining the functions of the cards and also to keep a sense of the humor of the game (it's much funnier to think of the cards as exploding kittens rather than bombs, for example).

The video clearly targets a Spanish-speaking viewer who has some English, but perhaps not enough to play the game without help. This fits with the overall sense that modern gaming culture has been imported into Mexico from the English-language discourse, even though some elements originated in Germany. This is supported by the fact that the video about *Catan* uses the English language version of the game, rather than the original *Die Siedler von Catan* (The Settlers of Catan).[19] *Catan* is much less language-dependent than *Exploding Kittens*, as it generally uses symbols rather than words, though some cards need explaining. Campos translates in this video the names of the cards with a Spanish phrase that is close in meaning to the English, for example, "Longest road" becomes "camino más largo" (longest road), while showing the card in English. This, again, helps Spanish-speaking viewers who have an English copy of the game and suggests that translanguaging is an important part of playing modern board games in Mexico (as it was in Colombia in Uribe-Jongbloed's account).

Boardgaming fan translation in this short example, then, is focused on making games accessible without necessarily translating the whole text. As such, it relies on the existing English-language knowledge of the viewers, which suggests that viewers already have some education in English and are happy to use it (and therefore it suggests a more middle-class viewer who has access to such education). The influence of English-language gaming culture is obvious, but this is also complemented with the promotion of Mexican board games. However, these games themselves are influenced by games in English (and other European languages), so this is not entirely a case of different paradigms of gaming, but of local and international productions.

These examples echo our discussion throughout the chapter of the necessity of situating analysis through the discussion of local conditions that surround the translation, as well as examining how those practices differ across locations. Focusing on languages other than English can help shift fan studies away from its focus on North America, and by studying fan practices outside of the Global North and outside of English, we can explore how fan cultures interact and creolize or react to each other, while also getting a better sense of how fandom functions more globally. This is fairer to fans worldwide and also constitutes an important step forward in the study of increasingly transcultural and translingual fan practices.

CHAPTER FOUR

Cosmopolitanism and Worldmaking in Queer Fan Translation

As we were writing this book, the film *I Saw the TV Glow* (Jane Schoenbrun, 2024) attracted our attention. Although at the time of writing it hadn't been officially released in the UK, and we hadn't had a chance to see it in full, it had just been released in the United States, and it was screened at Sundance in January 2024, so there were reviews available for several months before we started writing (e.g., Lee 2024), as well as a trailer online.[1] Something about the aesthetics of the film is particularly interesting and relevant to our discussion of queer fan translation in this chapter. The film itself deals with queerness, fandom, and identity, following the story of two viewers of a fictional sci-fi TV show called *The Pink Opaque* (the title of which we read as a clue to its queerness) who obsess over it in ways that feel familiar to TV fans in the 1990s, when videos of broadcasts were highly prized items and it was easy to miss an episode or two and therefore crucial plot points. The film connects queerness and fandom in interesting ways that are attractive to us as researchers on these topics.

The characters in *I Saw the TV Glow* bring to mind a quote from Eve Kosofsky Sedgwick:

> I think that for many of us in childhood the ability to attach intently to a few cultural objects, objects of high or popular culture or both, objects whose meaning seemed mysterious, excessive, or oblique in relation to the codes most readily available to us, became a prime resource for survival. We needed for there to be sites where the meanings didn't line up tidily with each other, and we learned to invest those sites with fascination and love. (Sedgwick 1994, 3)

The quote comes from an essay called "Queer and Now," which reflects on Sedgwick's trajectory in queer studies, and she later connects this "ardent reading" to queer experience (1994, 4). She could also be describing fandom more generally, understood as an affective bond with a text (as we discussed in Chapter 1), and, importantly, a fannish usage of cultural products as "goods to think with" (Martin 2017), that is, the way in which cultural products can be read in a way that allows us to reflect on our own lives. Exploring those "sites where the meanings didn't line up tidily with each other" opens up a number of intellectual and affective possibilities which allow viewers to reconsider or deepen their understanding of their own experience. This might take place in thoughts, in diaries, in fanfic or fanart, or in translational activities.

This use of media as goods to think with can be especially important to queer fans,[2] as they might not be in a situation where they can express their sexualities openly due to ongoing stigmas around homosexuality. No society is entirely free of heteronormativity, that is, the pressure to be heterosexual and form a monogamous couple. The LGBTQIA+ community can provide support, but not everyone has access to it (Driver 2007, 14). We can see this dynamic in the novel *The Miseducation of Cameron Post* (Danforth 2012): Cameron is attracted to girls but lives in a small town. She watches videos of films where there is some female same-sex desire as a way of thinking through her own sexuality. It is only when she meets Lindsey, on holiday from Seattle, that she begins to be connected to lesbian culture through Lindsey's recommendations and letters. As Susan Driver (2007, 14) argues, "Popular culture is . . . a process through which queer girls creatively imagine possibilities, forge connections, make meanings, and articulate relations." Queer fandom can be seen to be part of queer worldmaking (Berlant and Warner 1998), that is, connecting to a wider queer community and learning its codes and practices as well as imagining a queer space.[3] There is also an international and intercultural dimension to this worldmaking, which fan translation contributes to.

In this chapter, we examine queer fan practices before exploring how queer texts and ideas travel in translation. We analyze a fan translation of a reaction video to the Boys' Love/*danmei* cartoon *Heaven Official's Blessing 2* (2023) to illustrate how the craft of fan translation can lead to queer fan community discussion and negotiate queer cultures from around the world. As with the other chapters, fan translation is a transformative practice that encourages community and allows for the imprint of individual interpretation in the text.

Queer Fandoms

Gender and sexuality have been present in fan studies since the early 1990s (e.g., Bacon-Smith 1992, 228–54). We cannot, therefore, give an overview of all work on the topic; we can only highlight some of the key trends. The discussion of queer fandoms is further complicated, as Eve Ng and Julie Levin Russo (2017) note, by the fact that some work from film studies looks at queer audiences and makes queer readings of texts where queer topics have been hidden or censored, such as in Hayes Code era Hollywood films (White 1999). Clare Whatling (1997) makes the argument that lesbian viewing practices are what make lesbian films, rather than necessarily any overt lesbian representation in the film itself. Similar processes happen in gay male culture according to David Halperin (2012). This sort of audience-focused reading—which relies on the audience to determine whether or not a film or other object is perceived as gay, lesbian, or queer—demonstrates the ways in which viewers make meaning of films, which is similar to the meaning-making practices among fans.[4] The informal practices of queer cinema viewing in the mid-twentieth-century United States, which Ryan Powell (2019, 19–63) refers to as the "underground," also resemble later fan practices as they take place in a range of locations from bars to private homes for a small community of viewers. Yet these discussions are more clearly homed in film rather than fan studies, and they do not really use the same methodologies (ethnography, interviews, analysis of fan creations) that fan studies does (Ng and Russo 2017). However, they are useful for fan studies as they provide an understanding of how queer viewing can be practiced in relation to both visibly queer media and media which do not overtly refer to LGBTQIA+ characters.

Work on queer celebrity fandom (e.g., DeAngelis 2001; Zhao 2021) analyzes how queer audiences follow queer celebrities but also how straight celebrities are followed by queer audiences, highlighting how queer fandom may not be attached to overtly queer shows or celebrities. These fandoms contribute to the construction of a shared cultural space connected to non-heteronormative sexualities which could be understood as a form of worldmaking. However, queer fans are also aware that some media companies present texts as potentially queer to get a queer-identifying audience to engage with them, but without having overtly queer characters or storylines, a practice known as queerbaiting (Ng 2017; Brennan 2019). Queerbaiting acknowledges a queer audience while at the same undermining queer representation. Shows with LGBTQIA+ characters have become more mainstream in many places (Ng 2023), though far from all, and this has been changing the ways in which queer fandoms work as queer representation on screen becomes more prevalent and thus easier to access.[5]

One central practice in the research on queer fan studies is slash fanfic, which dates back to the 1970s. In slash, fan writers imagine a same-sex relationship between characters who, in the canon of the show, do not ostensibly have same-sex desires. The classic form of this is Kirk/Spock slash, with the term "slash" coming from the slash mark in the middle (Jenkins 1992, 186). Often slash has focused on male/male pairings; Ng and Russo (2017) note that femslash—slash about female same-sex relationships—has typically been "underrepresented" in the scholarship on slash, even though there is evidence for it existing since before the internet. As they point out, though, in many popular TV shows from before the 1990s there are seldom strong friendships between female characters which would serve as the basis for slash elaboration, in contrast to the strong male friendships in a show like *Star Trek*. For them, the watershed moment for femslash was *Xena: Warrior Princess* (1995–2001), which focused on the strong female character Xena and her companion Gabrielle; that is, it offered a strong female friendship to base the fanfic on. Shows like *Buffy the Vampire Slayer* (1997–2003) offered material for femslash writers (Ng and Russo 2017) as there were also strong female friendships and, in later seasons, lesbian characters. Some lesbian viewers found these shows empowering (Collier, Lumadue, and Wooten 2009), in ways similar to the lesbian (and queer readings more generally) we have already discussed.

Slash is, however, not straightforwardly queer. What complicates slash as a queer fandom is that many of the creators are actually straight women (Jenkins 1992, 191; Busse and Lothian 2018, 117), and it is difficult to know the sexual identities of people who read it, meaning that readers and writers may not themselves identify as queer. Some early slash fiction was criticized for avoiding or even rejecting gay culture and ignoring gay politics (Jenkins 2006a, 74–82; Busse and Lothian 2018, 120), though later work has been more attentive to this. At the same time, the bodies and sexualities in slash can be read as androgynous (Jenkins 1992, 193–8), meaning that it can also undermine gender perceptions and thus be read as queer. The focus on same-sex relationships, which were previously not so visible on mainstream television, also reinforces the queer reading of slash.

Where a great deal of slash reads in a queer way texts that do not have openly LGBTQIA+ characters—though there is some writing that also ships characters who are[6]—Boys' Love fandom focuses on a genre where the narratives themselves are focused on same-sex relationships between men. Boys' Love, known as *yaoi* in Japanese and *danmei* in Chinese, has active (heterosexual identifying) female fans, though, like slash, knowing the precise identities of who is reading it is difficult (for a summary of surveys, see Madill 2018, 130–1). We do not think that it can be viewed as solely a female-oriented genre, even if female fans are more visible: the representation of male–male desire still offers a queer potential. What is interesting about Boys' Love, in relation to our discussion elsewhere in this book, is that a good deal of the scholarship on it has investigated contexts outside of the usual Anglophone/Global North ones: as the genre originated in Japan, there is work on Japanese fans (Nagaike and Suganuma 2013), fans in greater China (Lavin, Yang, and Zhao 2017), in Asia more generally (Welker 2023), and in Thailand (Baudinette 2023), who all have different relationships with Boys' Love media and its transnational circulation. There is also Girls' Love, or *yuri*, which focuses on female–female relationships, but there is less scholarship on this (Friedman 2017), reflecting the sorts of gender imbalance seen with femslash (and more widely, lesbian media compared to gay male media).

While slash and BL are far from the only topics in queer fandom, they have been central to the scholarship. A smaller amount of work exists on trans fandom (Duggan and Fazekas 2023) and cross-gender cosplay (Chao 2017). The international aspects of queer fandom, as seen in the work on Boys' Love but also on intercultural fandoms of queer celebrities (Chin and Morimoto 2013, among others), highlight translation and the issues around translating queer material.

Queer Translation

There has been a growing body of work on queer translation studies since the late 1990s. Two early articles introduce some important ideas. The first is that understandings of queerness in the text may be changed in translation. Identities and practices will be negotiated in translation in order to relate to the culture of the language into which the text is translated (Harvey 1998). Queer ideas can pose problems for translators, as was the case of the examples of American gay fiction translated into French that Keith Harvey examines. He argues that France does not accept subcultural identities in the same way that the United States does, due to a universalist conception of the citizen (Harvey 1998, 311–12) and so changes were made in the translation that reflected this lack of acceptance of subcultures.

The other central idea is that translation itself can be a "political tool" (Keenaghan 1998, 274) to increase queer visibility and serve as an intervention in the culture it is being translated into. In fact, this is the reverse of the dequeering that can take place in other circumstances: translations can disrupt or acquiesce to local expectations, depending on what the translators want to achieve. Realistically, there is likely to be a combination of both approaches in the same translation as different aspects will call for different strategies, depending on the translator's own subjective choices, impositions from publishers, censorship, and so on. As we argued in Chapter 1, the interest in translation is understanding these choices in the text, how they have come about, and what effect they have.

The idea that translation forms a process of acceptance and resistance is expanded upon in Harvey's *Intercultural Movements: American Gay in French Translation* (2003), which examines in more depth how American gay fiction, as representative of or a synecdoche for American gay culture, was translated in France and how French gay culture reacted to it with a mix of rejection and acceptance. Harvey explores not just the translation of the language of the texts, especially the gayspeak (Hayes 1976) or stereotypical in-group language of gay men, but also how the covers of the translated text are used to frame a reading of the novels. Harvey's concern with how American gay (and more widely, queer) culture has been received in other cultures is echoed in work on the globalization of sexuality (Altman 2001; Binnie 2004), which explores how American queer community practices have become in many ways hegemonic, due in part to the international distribution of USAmerican queer media and queer theory.[7] Joseph Massad has pointed out the limitations of importing models that developed in the United States elsewhere, as Western models of homosexual identity led to increased attention and negative effects on men who have sex with men in Egypt (Massad 2002). Attitudes to same-sex attraction and sexual behavior, as well as gender variance, are quite culturally specific and relate to a mix of legal, historical, medical, religious, and other discourses and practices. This means that the translation of queer texts is always going to run into some sort of friction as there are always differences in culture that will affect it. Sometimes, this friction will be so severe that the text won't be officially translated, or the translation will be censored and overtly queer material removed. This happened when the Freddie Mercury biopic *Bohemian Rhapsody* (Bryan Singer, 2018) was translated into Chinese (Jin and Ye 2022), for example.

By exploring these sorts of differences between cultures, translation can become a type of queer methodology, as Evren Savcı (2021) argues. Drawing from the work of Naoki Sakai, Savcı positions translation as a social practice that mediates between cultures. She is interested in the ways in which the same term would have different meanings for different groups of people (Savcı 2021, 13), often in translation from English to Turkish but also within Turkish. She sees this as highlighting the historically bound yet changing nature of language and culture (2021, 14). Exploring translation offers Savcı a means to critique the English-language focus of queer theory and the limitations this poses to its way of knowing (she uses the term "epistemology," 2021, 12). Focusing on translations, then, illuminates how ideas spread and change and are adopted, appropriated, and resisted (often all at the same time).

In relation to how global sexuality studies has treated the cross-cultural movement of ideas about sexuality, Brian James Baer (2021, 55) argues that two positions are prevalent: total untranslatability ("radical alterity") and total translatability ("transposability"). He argues that this removes agency from translators, who may well be taking a path somewhere between these poles (2021, 59–60) through, for example, selectively using some terms or appropriating them for use in different cultures. Baer stresses how this can highlight the agency of translators in the Global South. To return to the notion of creolization that we borrowed from Shu-mei Shih and Françoise Lionnet (2011) in the previous chapter, the sorts of ideas about sexuality produced in this translational view end up being both local and global, both American and not; a creolizing of sexual knowledges as ideas and discourses interact. Translation is the practice that sits between cultures and discourse and so is where much of this creolization takes place.

While these approaches show the importance of translation for understanding sexualities in the global context, the work on queer translation remains quite limited. A significant amount of work on queer translation tends to focus on literary texts (Harvey 2003; Spurlin 2014; Epstein and Gillett 2017; Baer and Kaindl 2018; Baer 2021). There is a smaller but growing body of work on the translation of film and TV, including a monograph in Spanish (Martínez Pleguezuelos 2018) which analyzes the translation of American TV shows in Spain, and a special issue on translation and queer popular culture (Baldo, Evans, and Guo 2023). Other scholarship focuses on activist practices of translation (Baldo, Evans, and Guo 2021). A small group of works looks at the relationship between transgender and translation (Gramling and Dutta 2016; Robinson 2019). There is clearly more to do across genres and with different sexualities and agents. Fans are currently quite underrepresented in this scholarship.

Queer Fan Translations

There is surprisingly little research on queer fan translations. One area that has been studied, given its popularity in queer fandom, is the translation and dissemination of Boys' Love media. As it started as a phenomenon in Japan, early fans in China would translate it to make it available in Chinese, although locally produced work has become more popular over time (Yang and Xu 2017, 8–9). Fan translation groups still exist for BL comics, but use registration to avoid the commercial use of their work (Yang and Xu 2017). Moving away from more straightforward forms of fan translation, Ling Yang and Yanrui Xu (2017, 10) also discuss the ways in which Chinese fans will make use of Google Translate or other translation apps to read English-language materials, which would probably be categorized as "slash" rather than "Boys' Love." This exploration of fan writing in other languages exemplifies the strategies fans use to develop their own readings and understandings. As Bertha Chin and Lori Morimoto (2013, 98–9) have pointed out, "affinity" is a powerful element in such transcultural fandom practices, and the Chinese BL fans' translational readings of slash in English suggests an affinity between BL and slash.

Fan translation of queer media is often embedded within other queer community practices as we have discussed elsewhere (Guo and Evans 2020). In our study of the Chinese translation of Todd Haynes's *Carol* (2016) by the queer fansubbing group Jihua, we argued that fan translation was part of queer worldmaking, drawing on Lauren Berlant and Michael Warner's (1998) work. In other words, translation serves as part of the creation of a queer imaginative space as well as a loosely defined social space with shared references and understandings. This is especially the case in places where LGBTQIA+ media is censored, as in China. We found it to be the case for Jihua's work, which used *Carol* not just as an enjoyable film to watch (itself an important aspect of worldmaking) but also as an intervention in the discussion of lesbian and queer culture in China. This is seen also in their translations of relevant connected material, such as Heather Hogan's (2016) article about the lack of attention *Carol* received at the Oscars, which help to give a context for film and its reception. Choices in the translation itself, which Jihua revised, also showed the group putting their own interpretation into the text, demonstrating how translation stems from a (fan) reading of the text that does more than just work out what people are saying, but rather uses the text as part of a larger movement of worldmaking or discussion. In this example, then, queer fan translation is part of a wider queer fandom, which also makes texts accessible for other fans.

In some cases, fan translations compete with official ones. Giulia Magazzù (2023) examines how the official Italian dubs of the series *When We Rise* (2017) differ from the fan-produced subtitles. There are different affordances in dubbing and subtitling, that is, each has its own limitations as well as advantages in terms of length of speech, use of similar sounds, speed, and ease of understanding. This means comparing them will always show up some differences. Magazzù lists how the fan translation restored swearwords as well as more derogatory insults or offensive language. There is a move to a more literal translation (as we saw more generally in our discussion in Chapter 2) that makes the language feel more authentic and closer to what the characters are saying in English. Fan translators have more freedom to avoid the censorship that would come from broadcasting on TV, which would affect the official dubbing. The two translations coexisting show that fans are interested in the closer translation. Fan translation in this case does not make something available which previously wasn't, but rather offers a different interpretation of the text, reclaiming it as a queer text through the decisions made.

Heaven Official's Blessing Reaction Videos: Cosmopolitanism, Community, and Overcoming Censorship

To understand how fan translation can navigate intercultural queer understanding and develop queer community, we turn now to a case study of a Chinese fan's translation of a video of two Canadian queer fans reacting to the first episode of the recently released 天官賜福 (*tian guan ci fu*, hereafter TGCF)/*Heaven Official's Blessing* Season 2, an internationally popular Chinese *danmei* (Boys' Love) cartoon from 2023.[8] The two Canadian fans featured in the video are Kictor and their girlfriend, Stitch, who refer to themselves together as Stictor. Both of them are hard-core *Heaven Official's Blessing* fans and Kictor is particularly influential among the *Heaven Official's Blessing* fan community, with 124,000 followers on their YouTube channel about *danmei* works by Mo Xiang Tong Xiu (MXTX), a well-known Chinese *danmei* novelist. Although YouTube is banned in mainland China, many of Kictor's YouTube videos discussing *Heaven Official's Blessing* have been translated by Chinese *Heaven Official's Blessing* fans and circulated on Chinese social media platforms such as Bilibili, including the one we discuss. This example demonstrates the complexity of media circulation, moving from a Chinese text in English translation via a Canadian commentary on it to a new Chinese translation. It also demonstrates a cosmopolitan sensibility as it serves to link the Chinese *danmei* community to a wider group of global queer fans.

Before we enter into the details of this fan-translated video, it is important to note that the *Heaven Official's Blessing* cartoon series was adapted from a novel with the same name by MXTX. The novel, initially published as a series on the website Jinjiang Literature City (jjwxc.net)[9] in 2017 and 2018, centers on a romance between two young men, Xie Lian, who was a former prince of Xianle Kingdom before he became a god, and Hua Cheng, a Ghost King who has also a firm follower of Xie Lian since they encountered each other when Xie Lian was Xianle prince. The novel was immensely popular among *danmei* fans and has been disseminated in nine languages online via fan translations years before the official English translations were published in 2021.[10] This wide fan base has led to its commercialization through its cartoon adaptation, comics, and audio drama.[11] The first season of the cartoon adaptation was simulcast on Bilibili and Funimation in 2020 and then in Netflix in 2021 with subtitles in seven languages and distribution in thirty-six countries.[12] The second season was first broadcast in October 2023 on crunchyroll.com and Bilibili in Hong Kong, Macao, and Taiwan, but at the time of writing it is not officially accessible in mainland China. This inaccessibility is one of the reasons why fan reaction videos to *Heaven Official's Blessing* Season 2 were chosen to be translated by Chinese fans, especially given the fact that these videos include a window showing the cartoon that the fans are watching and the reactions are carefully placed in-between the pause and replay of the show without overtaking or erasing the audio of the cartoon. The reaction videos thus provide the latest information about the series that others are eager to know about but have no access to, which fits into a typical pattern of fan translations being undertaken to offer access to a text (see Chapter 2). As seen in Figure 4.1, the reaction video was visually presented with the screen split: the left side shows the Stictor couple watching the anime with their earphones and chatting to each other; the right presents the anime on their screen.

Both parts are translated by a Chinese fan (hereafter F), with the Chinese subtitles on the top and the English at the bottom in each window. Therefore, viewers who have limited knowledge of English language can understand both the English dubbed show and Stictor's conversation in English. The double-layered translation is effective in terms of clarifying the various reactions (e.g., shock, hand covering mouth, laugh) of the couple; it also provides space for the fan translator to interpret both the English dubbing and Stictor's reactions.

FIGURE 4.1 Heaven Official's Blessing © *Bilibili Co., Ltd. 2020–2.*
*"HEAVEN OFFICIAL'S BLESSING SEASON 2 EPISODE 1
REACTION! #tgcf"* © *Kictor 2024.*

For example, there is one scene in the Great Martial
Hall where General Pei Ming accuses Xie Lian of having
"suspicious" connections with the Ghost King, Hua Cheng,
in front of all the gods, including Jun Wu, the Heavenly
Emperor. The Wind Master questions him: "Are you saying
Princess Xian Le (Xie Lian) colluded with a Ghost King?"
(Translated by F as 你是想说仙乐太子勾结鬼王?). Xie Lian
adds, "Do I know them?" (translated by F as 我认识祂吗?).
Here, F translates "them" into "祂," a rare variant of the third-
person singular pronoun 他 (*ta*), with the same pronunciation
but referring specifically to God in the Chinese translation of
Bible, with a note under the Chinese subtitle explaining "them
不是'他们' 而是作为非二元性别常用代词" ("them" here
is not the usual "they" but a common non-binary personal
pronoun). This note explains Stictor's reactions in the video:
they pause, look at each other, and unanimously speak the
word "them," and Kictor follows up by commenting that the
English dubber and subtitle editor "James Cheek wins every
award to ever award ever."[13] It is also through this note that
the fan translator introduces to other Chinese fans the use

of the English words "they/them" in current media discourse to emphasize diversity and inclusiveness. This additional information provided by F is clearly appreciated by other fans and also encouraged them to pay close attention to the nuanced use of personal pronouns and the LGBTQIA-friendly English dubbing. For example, one fan immediately commented "啊啊哈哈哈哈没有直接用he" (Ah ah ha ha ha ha [the English dubbing] didn't directly use "he") in the bullet subtitles (*danmaku*) on the top of the screen. Another comment pointed out that the Wind Master—who is a man but likes to transform into a woman—was referred to as "she/her" in the English dubbing, stirring up a discussion among fans in the *danmaku* about the gender-free Chinese third personal pronouns (他/她) which have the same pronunciation *ta* and why the use of "she" actually fits better with the Wind Master's image and explains Xie Lian's confusion when he encountered the he/him version of the Wind Master later. This discussion is interesting not only because it exemplifies how translation helps develop fans' sensitivity to gender-inclusive language but also because it demonstrates how the explicit references to sexuality and gender in the English dubbing can be made less explicit and, yet, at the same time highlighted through fans' creative translation strategy, drawing viewers' attention for close reading.

Making queer terms less explicit is attributable to China's strict censorship of homosexual-themed content (including *danmei*) on Chinese social media platforms. While homosexuality has not been illegal in China since 1997, it is still a sensitive topic subject to stringent surveillance, being targeted in the government's "cleansing" campaigns aiming to crack down on "obscene" content in the past decade (Zhang 2017, Zhao et al. 2017). The "responsibility" policy that the Chinese government recently carried out has also forced Chinese internet intermediaries, for example, social media platforms, to assist this censorship, making it more difficult for Chinese *danmei* fans to discuss or post anything explicitly related to homosexuality, especially given the government's ban on *danmei*-themed media adaptations in 2021

(Zheng 2024). To circumvent the censorship, Chinese *danmei* fans have developed coded forms of expression (e.g., *shehui zhuyi xiongdi qing*, 社会主义兄弟情, socialist brotherhood) to engage with their favorite texts (Ng and Li 2020). In the video we are discussing, although "祂" (*ta*, they) hasn't become a widely accepted code for non-binary personal pronoun among Chinese fans, its rare use in modern Chinese language makes it prominent in the translation, inviting further interpretations from viewers. Similar practices can be found in F's translation of the sentence "His gay little like, his villainous like, ['Oh, anyways']" Rather than translating the English word "gay" into 同性恋 (*tongxinglian*), the established Chinese translation for homosexuality, or keeping it in English, also a widely accepted practice within Chinese LGBTQIA+ communities (which is also used in this video in other examples), F translated into "他那种给里给气的坏水" (He is that kind of gayish villain), in which the word "gay" is transliterated as 给 (*gei*, same pronunciation as gay but means "to give"), an expression recreated from the Chinese idiom 痞里痞气(*pi li pi qi*, slovenly) and widely used within Chinese LGBTQIA+ communities, referring to non-masculine behavior that is identified with gay men. These indirect translations of nonnormative gender and sexualities are part of the fan translator's strategies to get their translation past the platform's content algorithms and avoiding attracting unwanted attention from the censors. On the other hand, they also mirror the playfulness of fan translation in finding ways to circumvent censorship and engage with the queer readings offered by other non-Chinese fans. Quite a few viewers noticed the "nuanced" translation, with some praising the funny translation and some providing more direct translation in the comments. F then responded that those punch lines in the translation were added deliberately by themselves, as they had so much fun and were laughing along with Stictor while translating this video so they wanted to make translation as "有意思" (interesting, funny).

If designing their own punch lines is part of the fun that F had in their translation of this video, another important part is to share their enjoyment of viewing Stictor's queer

interpretations of Jun Wu's (the Heavenly Emperor) father/
son bond with Xie Lian in this episode. This queer pairing
is clearly new to Chinese fans, with many fans starting to
ask for confirmation in the *danmaku* or expressing their
enjoyment in reading this interpretation. F clearly predicted
these reactions and provided details to highlight and explain
those oblique lines in the English dubbing. For example,
in the scene when Jun Wu said that he has built a new
temple for Xie Lian so he can have a decent place for his
followers to worship him, Stictor got extraordinarily excited
and shouted, "Oh no, oh no," because the English dubbing
used "erected" rather than "built." Apart from explaining
Stictor's reactions, F's translation is also adjusted to express
their own excitement and eagerness to share with other
fans: for example, not only was the English word "erected"
underlined in the subtitle, but the note in square bracket
explaining "erect 除了有建立的意思 还有勃起的意思" (the
word "erect," apart from meaning build, also refers to boner)
(see Figure 4.2).

FIGURE 4.2 Heaven Official's Blessing © *Bilibili Co., Ltd. 2020–2.*
*"HEAVEN OFFICIAL'S BLESSING SEASON 2 EPISODE 1
REACTION! #tgcf"* © *Kictor 2024.*

This excitement is continued in the comments section where F actively engaged with other fans who shared their appreciation and enjoyment in seeing the new pairing of Jun Wu and Xie Lian by Stictor. In fact, among the 203 comments on this post,[14] seventy-five are F's replies to other fans, many of which echo others' excitement and enjoyment of this new queer reading. It is through these interactions that issues such as censorship and LGBTQIA+ visibility are further explored, demonstrating the interlocking of fan and queer communities. While some fans who self-identified as "rotten girls" (a term referring to female fans of Boys' Love media) in their comments expressed their "jealousy" of the English audience who are able to consume such explicit *danmei* in English dubbing, others went further and reflected on why these changes occurred in English dubbing and how to foster structural change in China. For example, one viewer self-claimed as "钛合金钢铁直男" (Titanium steel straight man, hereafter T) commented that he thoroughly enjoyed this translated reaction video and felt that censorship of *danmei* works such as *Heaven Official's Blessing* is really unnecessary, especially given that homosexuality has long existed in Chinese society, and it is part of Chinese culture that needs to be represented and understood by others. T further added that more consumers and more discussions of Chinese *danmei* works would eventually lead to changes of censorship. T's comment made an effective connection with F, who responded in a few minutes, admitting how touched they were when they were understood and supported by others who are outside of the *danmei* community.

This example, then, demonstrates the community- and world-making potential of fan translation through the way that the translated version attracted comments, both in the comments section and as *danmaku*, that served to create discussion around queer topics such as the use of non-binary pronouns. The creative choices of the translator also demonstrate adaptations made to deal with censorship which also allow for and encourage further discussion. At the same time, the translation allows Chinese fans to engage with a queer reading by Canadian fans and thus get a different cultural interpretation. Whether or not these are the most accurate translations is beside the point: they serve as a form of cultural intervention that generates discussion, while also linking fans across national borders. This may only be a short example, but it shows the potential for fan translation to be relevant to wider discussions of queer culture in a global context.

CHAPTER FIVE

Conclusion

Fan Translation and the Changing Face of Global Media Distribution

In our local suburban chain bookstore in a mall on Glasgow's Southside, there is a whole wall of translated Japanese comics. It's three times larger than the graphic novels section (i.e., comics that are not translated) and about the same size as the Young Adult section. This is fairly common in bookstores across the UK now, but is something that we would not have imagined as teenagers in the 1990s, when translated manga was sometimes available in comic book stores but seldom in mainstream bookshops. Similarly, a cursory search through Netflix brings up a large number of translated Japanese cartoons, which thirty years ago would have been unthinkable. But there's not only Japanese anime, there's also K-drama, a seemingly complete collection of *Star Trek* shows, cult TV and films from the United Kingdom and United States, as well as a wider range of international media. There's stuff here that it would have been difficult to find when we were younger, but which is now a few clicks away. There are whole libraries of content on the other streaming services as well as on YouTube or Bilibili, both of which carry enormous quantities of translated media, often including unofficial versions (including fan translations).

Our point is that there is now far more cult and translated (and translated cult) media easily available than ever before. This contrasts with the idea that Anglophone cultures are typically averse to translations—it's often quoted that around 3 percent of all book publications in English are translations (Three Percent n.d.), though this is also changing (Flood 2016). Yet this abundance of easy-to-find, (professionally) translated materials also seems to conform to the logic of the fan translations we saw in Chapter 2: making available a huge amount of content and finding out things that had not been distributed previously. Not only the quantity of material, in different genres and from different locations, but also the fact that the texts are available with their original language soundtrack, subtitles, and often dubbing, fits this same logic. There is now a choice of how you watch a show or movie and more chance to hear the original voices, if you so choose, or you could choose a dubbed version if you preferred that. This tendency is increased once you look at specialized services like Crunchyroll (which is not available in the UK) which offer vast libraries of anime. The archival function of Disney+, which gives you access to a large amount of Disney's back catalog (though not all of it), also fits with a fan logic: it gives access to older series that it would have been hard to see all of when they were on broadcast TV and allows viewers to dig out old gems.

There are also similar moves in other media, drawing from the affordances of digital distribution, such as the online comics platform ComiXology, which is now part of Amazon. This gives access to a wide range of comics, including translated titles (especially manga). The various official game platforms, such as Nintendo's eShop, have also made available older games, while the mini-consoles, such as the SNES mini or the PC Engine mini, appeal to retro gaming fans and fan archiving, although they did not include new translations (interestingly, the PC Engine mini—known as the TurboGrafx-16 mini in the United States—did include games only in Japanese). It's clear that companies have been listening to and watching fans, as Henry Jenkins (2006b) noted they were starting to earlier in the 2000s: more material from around the world is available in translation than ever before.

So, have fan translators won?

It depends on what you think they were trying to win. If, like Alyssa Tremblay (2018, 329), you think that fan translators are motivated by the "desire to obtain and consume the product as soon as possible," then it would seem that the current media smorgasbord of international content on streaming or other platforms would serve that purpose. There is so much material, often released at the same time as in its country of origin, that there is no need to seek it out anymore. With the possibility of both subtitles and dubbing, there isn't the competition between an official format using one modality and an unofficial format using another, as there previously was in Italy, for example (Massidda 2015). This increasing amount of available material follows patterns already seen with DVDs, especially for anime (Denison 2015, 102–10). Of course, this only refers to media texts—film and TV—rather than the wider field of texts that can be translated. Fan translators of popular literature, especially of web literature (i.e., writing i.e., produced for distribution and reading on the internet), are still working (Wu 2021) as there is little capital behind this sort of text that could pay for translations.[1] Similarly, there will continue to be a need for fan translation of song lyrics, as people want to know what songs in other languages are about, and there is no one way to do that otherwise given the general lack of official translations. Importantly, such translations are supplementary to the song: they don't compete with it in a market but enhance people's enjoyment of the song and as such work as a process of promotion rather than replacement.

There is also evidence that video games are more typically using a sim-ship model, that is, they are released (in translation) globally (Yang 2021) rather than in one country or region at a time, as used to happen. This also gives a sense that companies are more aware of the international markets for their products and are trying to reduce lag between destinations. Given the high costs of creating AAA games (high-budget games usually produced and distributed by major companies)—recently estimated to be around US$200 million, up from US$50–150 million in 2018 (Zollner 2023)—you can understand why games companies want to reach as many customers as possible as quickly as possible. Yet a lot of fan translation of video games was always of older games that had not been released internationally (O'Hagan and Mangiron 2013, 301), so in this case, while new material is shipping quicker, fan translators still have older materials to work with.[2]

Focusing on just accessing material and making that material available to others relies on quite an instrumental understanding of translation, that is, an understanding that translation is just a means to the end of accessing texts.[3] Translation, as we have argued throughout this book, is more than this: translation is an interpretative and creative act. It actively transforms materials through translators' interpretations. It has its own rewards as an activity: translating can be a pleasurable experience in itself. We linked this in Chapter 2 to the idea of translation being a craft, that is, "good work for its own sake" (Sennett 2008, 20). Translation can be a slow, careful, mindful engagement with a text that includes deep reading and reflection. In this sense, the ready availability of many media texts in translation does not satisfy the itch to translate. There is a risk that such availability will reduce or eradicate fan translation of media texts, as there is already an existing translation and no perceived need for fan translation, as might the ready availability of machine translations from large language models (e.g., generative AI systems) or dedicated machine translation systems. Yet fans might continue to translate manually despite the alternative of official or machine translation, as translation allows fans to put their own stamp on texts, as well as reading them closely. In other words, the craft element of translating is a reason to do it.

On the other hand, Mel Stanfill has written about how, given the changes in media industry attitudes to fandom, which are becoming more accepting and tolerating, there are some fandom practices that are encouraged and others that are discouraged (Stanfill 2019, 10). She argues that fandom practices based on consumption, such as buying merch or following new series using the same IP (intellectual property), are preferred by media companies because they don't challenge or undermine the image of the product (Stanfill 2019, 77–103). Practices like fan fic—especially of the slash variety—or fan art or fan translation, which can repurpose and offer new interpretations of a text that challenge canon, are thus discouraged. One way to reduce the worries about fan translation is to render it seemingly redundant by making texts easily available in translation. Yet this doesn't explain why fan translation groups retranslate texts in order to bring to the fore their own interpretation or to reclaim the text, as we discussed in Chapter 4 (see Guo and Evans 2020; Magazzù 2023). This sort of activity makes clearer the interpretative and transformative nature of fan translation and seems less easy to stifle, though copyright law can be used to remove such retranslations from video-sharing websites.

In terms of the translation industry, there has been considerable disruption in recent years. Most of that disruption is coming from new technologies, such as neural machine translation and translation management platforms (Sakamoto, Evans, and Torres Hostench 2018), rather than fan translation, as was predicted in the earlier days of writing about fan translation (Pérez-González and Susam-Saraeva 2012, 151). In fact, neural machine translation—that is, machine translation that also incorporates machine learning or Artificial Intelligence (Kenny 2018)—has proved to be a very disruptive technology for the translation industry (O'Hagan 2016, 930).[4] Machine translation has become more central in the industry, with a shift toward postediting, that is, the editing of machine translation output, rather than fully human translation in many cases (Nunes Viera, Alonso, and Bywood

2019), though not all: machine translation poses problems for any sort of confidential document due to information not being kept confidential as it has to go into the machine translation system, most of which are now cloud-based (i.e., are accessed over the internet). Machine translation is also not really all that useful for forms of translation that require significant creativity, such as advertising. There is some debate about the usefulness of it for literary translation: in a recent article, Christophe Declercq and Guys-Walt van Egdom (2023, 55–7) note how machine translation can increase access to literatures in different languages, especially smaller languages, and thus alter global understandings of literature, but also risks missing out on nuances and flattening out cultural differences. Similar points could be made about the subtitling of media products based on automatic transcription and translation.

However, we think this debate overlooks a couple of important things: (1) having access to a text in translation is not the same as that text having been published in translation and (2) literary texts, and cultural texts more widely, are not the same as informative texts. Publishers are still going to look at whether or not something is saleable, and while the translation cost might be lower, there's still no guarantee that there will be any interest in publishing more translations. The second point is more complex: literary texts, like other cultural items such as film, video games, or art, are created by humans and do more than just provide information. Their meaning is not solely contained in their surface content—a fact attested to by fans' behavior as much as any scholarly reading. *Star Trek*, to take a classic example, is not just a story about a spaceship and its crew: it also offers models of friendship, entertainment of an evening, comfort against the vicissitudes of daily life, an example of a split infinitive, boredom, and many other things. Fans value this. Casual viewers get this. Machines do neither. Just as we have argued throughout this book that the interest in translation lies in its interpretative nature and thus the human intervention that is inherent to it, the interest in literary and media texts lies in their humanness, and the messy network of human interactions around them.[5]

There is more to localizing texts than just language. As Casey Brienza (2016, 9) argues in relation to manga, but the point holds for other cultural texts, "cultural flow can only be achieved through an active, labor-intensive, and oft-contested process." She prefers to call this "domestication" rather than "translation" or "localization," though we think both of these terms are apt and would shy away from "domestication" given the theorizing of it as an ethnocentric form of translation by Lawrence Venuti (1995). Just slapping a translation on a text is not the same as considering how it needs to be adapted or altered for local audiences, processes that Brienza explores in her book. Fan translators are often aware of this and are involved in these larger processes, with some of their decisions influencing translators of official versions, according to interviews with Brienza (2016, 117).

Beyond the anecdotal evidence of such interviews, it's not always clear what influence fan translators have had on the translation industry. The widened range of media available over streaming is as much a consequence of the affordances of the platforms as it is a reflection of hunger for international content. It's been documented that in film distribution, some fans have become distributors (Crisp 2015, 43), and there is also anecdotal evidence of fan translators becoming professionals (Mandelin 2013; see also O'Hagan and Mangiron 2013, 309–10) but, as far as we are aware, no large-scale study. It was suggested that fansubbing would become a training ground for translators (O'Hagan 2008) but there is little evidence, beyond the anecdotal, to support that. The sorts of translation techniques highlighted by Abé Mark Nornes (1999), like the use of headnotes or visual creativity, have not become mainstream. There have been some moves to using more creative subtitling techniques, but more within the storytelling of non-translated shows than in translations. For example, the BBC show *Sherlock* (2010–17) used on-screen text to illustrate the central character's thinking, such as his decoding of a message in German (Pérez-González 2014, 270–5). While this is an interesting use of on-screen text that challenges TV narrative conventions, there is little to link it to fansubbing other than some visual similarities. The use of colors in subtitles, for different characters, has long been standard in TV subtitling (in the UK at least). It is not very clear if there has been any significant influence on conventional subtitling from fansubbing.

So it seems that the influence of fan translation is contestable at best: more things are being translated, but that might just be a realization that there is a market for translated materials and it might be caused by the greater capacity in streaming. In other fields, there is even less hard data. In the rest of this chapter, we want to explore briefly how media companies have tried to use fan translations and translators. We focus on film and TV distribution, as this is the most visible area where this has happened.

Platforming Fans

The use of fansubbing by Rakuten Viki has been studied by several scholars (Dwyer 2012, 2017, 164–84; Henthorn 2019; Zhang 2022). It is the one platform that has really taken fan translation to heart. However, it has been noted that more recently, the emphasis on fan translation has been pushed away from its landing page to the "Community" tab, which de-emphasizes it (Choi, Kim, and Evans 2023, 322). If you click on any of the current shows, it does tell you who has translated them, and there is an invitation to join the community. It is difficult to tell from the website, though, how many people only watch the TV shows. Existing scholarship suggests not that many translate compared to the amount of users of the website as a streaming service (Dwyer 2017, 166). But the community aspect of Viki still runs in the background (Dwyer 2017, 173–82) and is still very present on the current version of the website, even if it is not immediately foregrounded on the landing page. Viki remains unique in this model, though, and this can be traced to its origins as a "not-for-profit class project based around language learning" (Dwyer 2017, 165). The fan and community aspect has always been part of it, and this is something that other platforms have not been able to copy.

They have tried to, unsuccessfully. In 2017, Netflix set up project HERMES, which aimed to recruit subtitlers and localizers through standardized testing.[6] Netflix claimed at the time that

> We're quickly approaching an inflection point where English won't be the primary viewing experience on Netflix, and HERMES allows us to better vet the individuals doing this very important work so members can enjoy their favorite TV shows and movies in their language. (Fettner and Sheehan 2017a)

Viewing Netflix as multilingual, with English as a common but not majority experience, demonstrates an understanding of both markets and producers as global, rather than more Anglo-centric approaches to media (see our discussion in Chapter 3). Further detail on the actual process of HERMES testing was available on the Netflix technical blog (Fettner and Sheehan 2017b): besides testing how well potential translators would translate idioms, the plan was to keep a record of each translator's performance, rather than solely the performance of the agency they worked for. This collapsed very quickly— after just over a year—as Netflix found that it could not source and manage translators as well as its usual suppliers, that is, translation and localization agencies (Bond 2018). In fact, it was the popularity of the platform that made it unusable: too many people signed up (Bond 2018). While this is more an example of crowdsourcing than fan translation, as it did not solely rely on fan translation and it seems Netflix hoped to recruit professionals as well as amateurs, we would suggest that it also aimed to capitalize on fansubbing cultures through recruiting fansubbers who thought they would be as good as professionals.

Crowdsourcing translation has been successfully used by some organizations (e.g., TED, see O'Hagan 2016) and even Facebook (O'Hagan 2016), but it was clearly not suitable for Netflix. One obvious reason for this is that Netflix has quite strict standards for subtitling, with published guides for many languages.[7] The fact that they highlighted idioms and the problems they pose in their blogpost (Fettner and Sheehan 2017b) demonstrates they were aware of the decision-making needed in translation and that translation is both interpretative and context-dependent. Their examples included "made a killing" (i.e., did really well) and "hit the road" (leave). Entering these phrases into Google Translate gives fairly literal translations that do not reflect the idiomatic meanings.[8] Being able to translate idioms is only one part of the skill set of subtitlers, though, which also includes segmentation of the text, making the subtitles fit the space available, timings, and so on. While fansubbers do all these things, they do not always do them in the same way as professional subtitlers, meaning that fansubbing practices are not simply exchangeable for professional practices.[9]

If crowdsourcing proved not to be a straightforward way of engaging fan expertise for Netflix, Asian platforms have come up with a technology that is arguably fan-oriented: *danmaku.*[10] *Danmaku* are comments that are projected on top of the video clip. They began on Nico Nico Douga (nicovideo .jp) in 2006 (Yang 2020, 256) and spread to Chinese sites like Bilibili and also to Viki (Dwyer 2017, 168). The experience of viewing a video with *danmaku* can be somewhat frustrating, as heavily commented videos can be covered by the comments themselves (Chen, Gao, and Rau 2017, 736). What *danmaku* allow is for the video to become a social space, as if watching with other people who are chatting about it at the same time, somewhat like the fan club viewings that we started out with in Chapter 1 (Jenkins 1992, 76). In fact, users of *danmaku* have said this social aspect is one of their attractions (Chen,

Gao, and Rau 2017, 735). Users can comment on whatever they feel like as they watch and it offers an on-screen moment of connection with other users. At particularly funny or poignant moments, there tend to be more *danmaku* as more people are commenting.

As we saw in our discussion of *Heaven Official's Blessing* in Chapter 4, *danmaku* commentators sometimes comment on the translation, but comments on screen can also contain translations, as noted by Yuhong Yang (2020). The barrier to entry for people to contribute such translations is very low, even compared to other forms of fan translation: all you need to do is use the interface (Yang 2020, 265). While Bilibili provides etiquette guides (Yang 2020, 268), people may not follow them. There is no guarantee of quality or even of the correctness of translations, again like the shouting out of comments in Jenkins's example. This brings back a form of anarchic practice to *danmaku* that has been eroded in the safer practices of organized fan translation (as we discussed in Chapter 2). There is even a name for *danmaku* writers: "wild caption-*kun*" (Yang 2020). *Danmaku* are certainly much wilder translations than the domesticated offerings required by Netflix.[11] This gives *danmaku* translations a feeling of being more like other fan practices as a social activity that can create community. However, it should be noted that the community for *danmaku* is always virtual: *danmaku* are anonymized (unlike comments on the platform Viki), so it is impossible to know who wrote them, and, unlike the fan club screenings, you can't socialize in real life with other *danmaku* writers after the event.

Perhaps this rewilding of fan translation in the media will help to bring attention back to it and the possibilities it offers. It is, after all, a social activity that offers different ways of approaching a text. If translation is understood as an interpretative and transformative act, it can sit alongside other practices in fandom, as it shares being an interaction and an interpretation. While we've focused on media translation here, the fields of songs, games, and fan fic translation offer more examples of such wild fan practices that can broaden the understanding of fan translation and bring people together to discuss it.

Danmaku also highlight an ambiguity in fan translation more generally: it is both a creative activity that encourages community building, and at the same time, a way of making people stay on a platform by increasing engagement. It seems to both escape from capitalist goals and be enmeshed in them. This ambiguity is due to the fact that most fan translation takes place in corporate spaces—for example, on YouTube or Bilibili—and so serves those corporations. Even when it takes place on less-monetized websites, there is still the issue that most of the texts translated are popular culture texts that are themselves products of corporate enterprises.

The question of how to navigate this ambiguity remains open, especially as fan translation does not mirror other DIY (do-it-yourself) cultures that offer spaces for nonprofessional creativity, as it does not have a typically anti-corporate stance (Spencer 2008; Dale 2012). One way that we think offers a way out of the dualistic thinking of individual creativity/corporate profit, which itself does not take into account the various ways in which subcultures are always entangled with the corporate world, even if they reject it, is to approach fan translation from the angle of worldmaking. What sort of worlds do fan translators create through their translations and the interactions, in comments or *danmaku,* around them? How do they use mass media and mass culture to create a space for themselves, or to understand their own lives and the world around them? We think that asking these questions of fan translations—and fandom more generally—would help to highlight their importance as a way of engaging not just with media but the world.

We have argued throughout this book for a transformative understanding of translation that sees it as interpretative and creative. We have thus argued, through our discussion of the scholarship but also through our examples, that translation ought to be understood alongside and as part of fan practices.

Our third and fourth chapters demonstrated how fan translation can take place in fragmentary forms, as in the board game reviews, and also in newer genres like reaction videos. These examples also showed how fan translations could link communities together. Importantly, we've shown how fan translation can help make fan studies more multilingual and global. Finally, we have shown how newer forms of fan translation, such as those in *danmaku*, bring back a wildness to fan translation that can revitalize it. We hope that we have inspired readers to go beyond what they've read here and explore fan translations themselves. What other goal could a fandom primer have?

NOTES

Chapter 1

1 Umberto Eco criticizes Jakobson's definition of translation as it has the potential to confuse interpretation (as in any form of understanding) and translation (Eco 2003, 123–32). This is something we see in the openness of intersemiotic translation, which could include almost any interpretation in another medium.

2 It is worth noting that this understanding of translation is actually historically bound, and translators in the Middle Ages or in other times and places might not have understood translation in the same way. See Sakai (2006) for a theoretically nuanced exploration of what he calls the current "regime of translation."

3 It is beyond our scope here to cover the history of translation studies as a whole: there are now several introductory books to the field (e.g., Munday, Pintos Ramo, and Blakesley 2022; Pym 2023) as well as work on its history (Lange, Monticelli, and Rundle 2024).

Chapter 2

1 It should be noted that the two scholars know each other and teach together at the Baker Centre Research Summer School for Media Translation and Digital Culture. They did try to avoid overlap between the two entries.

2 Another term that aims to clarify different types of translation practice is "online collaborative translation" (Zwischenberger 2022), which is used to refer to online translation practices ranging from crowdsourcing to fan translation and also includes various forms of community translation practice,

which might be used for crisis communication or translation of sites such as Wikipedia. Again, fan translation is just one type of online collaborative translation, and it should be noted that fan translation need not be online or collaborative. The first recorded fansubs, for instance, are dated to 1986 (Leonard 2005, 291), that is, before the internet became public.

3   However, the term "user-generated" usefully links O'Hagan's discussion to wider currents in media studies discussing other user-generated practices in the cultural industries (e.g., Hesmondhalgh 2010).

4   Michael Cronin tried early on to capture some of these issues in his *Translation in the Digital Age* (2013), but from our perspective, the lack of interaction with work in media and cultural studies in that book feels like an obvious omission, especially given that the many issues that come about from the digitalization of translation were being discussed in relation to media in the 2000s (e.g., Deuze 2007).

5   There is a growing literature on such translation, much of which deals with nonprofessional translators in fields such as healthcare or with child language brokers, that is, children interpreting for their parents (Antonini et al. 2017). Even within work on media translation, fans are seldom the focus of research on nonprofessional practices (e.g., Antonini and Bucaria 2016), though they are more central in Orrego-Carmona and Lee (2017). People have different reasons for translating and collapsing all forms of nonprofessional translation together overlooks the different motivations as well as necessarily different practices.

6   The standard textbook on subtitling is Díaz-Cintas and Remael 2021 (which revises an older text from 2007). The constraints referred to in this paragraph are discussed there.

7   Douglas Schules (2014) extends this argument by proposing that the strategies used in anime fansubbing are constitutive of subcultural capital as they demonstrate the translator's knowledge of Japanese culture, as well as allowing viewers to develop their own.

8   Matt Hills (2017) argues a similar point and links fansubbing to neoliberal practices such as self-branding and "competitive entrepreneurial practice."

9 Nornes (2007, 188–228) also offers a useful examination of the process of dubbing.

10 *What's Up Tiger Lily* takes a Japanese spy film (*Kokusai himitsu keisatsu: Kagi no kagi/International Secret Police: Key of Keys*, Senkichi Taniguchi 1965) and replaces the Japanese dialogue with a comedic script written by Woody Allen and acted by American actors. *Can Dialectics Break Bricks?* takes a Hong Kong martial arts film (*Tongsau toikyundou/Crush*, Guangqi Tu 1972) and replaces the Cantonese dialogue with French dialogue that is inspired by the post-Marxist political writings of the Internationale Situationniste, whose members included theorists such as Guy Debord and Raoul Vaneigem.

11 Romhacking can also refer to nonlinguistic hacks such as redesigning levels (e.g., Newman 2018).

12 The official link for the British law is: https://www.legislation.gov.uk/ukpga/1988/48/contents. For the American law: https://www.copyright.gov/title17/. When citing the laws, we refer to these documents. We should make clear that our discussion does not constitute legal advice on these matters.

13 We are using the 1979 amendment of the Berne Convention, available here: https://www.wipo.int/wipolex/en/text/283698. We do not have space to go into changes made in the 100+ year history of the convention. For a critical history of US copyright law, see Vaidhyanathan (2001). For detailed work on international copyright law, see Ricketson and Ginsburg (2022).

14 Copyright has been discussed in translation studies. For a critical overview, see Lee (2020).

15 Information about the DSA in this chapter is taken from the European Commission's webpages, here and links: https://commission.europa.eu/strategy-and-policy/priorities-2019-2024/europe-fit-digital-age/digital-services-act_en.

16 We follow Venuti (2019) in using the term "instrumental" and opposing it to a more interpretative approach.

17 The research for this book was approved by the College of Arts Research Ethics Committee at the University of Glasgow, Application Number 100230058.

18 We have suggested that translation be understood as craft elsewhere: Guo and Evans (2020) and Evans (2022). However, in both those essays we only mentioned it very briefly.

Chapter 3

1 Thanks to Rowan Guo Evans for bringing this show to our attention.

2 After we submitted the first draft of this book, the journal *Transformative Works and Cultures* published an article entitled "Fan Studies in Latin America: A Call to Arms" (Amaral et al. 2024) which argued for more focus on Latin American fans in fan studies and also gave a useful overview of existing work in that region.

3 Rukmini Pande's (2016) chapter on race and fandom mentions Bollywood and critiques the US-centric nature of some fan studies work, so it could also be included in this group, although it does not specifically look at fans working in other languages.

4 Sociolinguistics studies the relationship between language and community (e.g., Llamas and Watt 2009).

5 This is a good reason to encourage language learning among fan and media scholars. Machine translation would work to an extent but is seldom effectively readable over article or book length.

6 For instance, race has not really been the topic of much theorizing in translation studies until recently, and the one monograph on the topic stays focused on the USAmerican context (Tachtiris 2024, 23).

7 Pascale Casanova (1999) makes this argument with more detail in relation to literature.

8 As discussed in Chapter 2, there is a reasonable body of material on fan translation in China. Our example in Chapter 4 will also relate to China; here we felt that Latin America and Africa were the areas most overlooked by the existing scholarship. There is also little research on fan translation in India.

9 Spanish and Portuguese are both grammatically gendered languages, and so the variations here are both the masculine and feminine endings. Non-binary endings are possible—*aficionadx* or *aficionad@*, for example—but are not always used. In relation to the term(s) *latino/a/x*, see Báez (2018), especially footnote 1.

10 Thanks to Ernesto Priego for bringing this database to our attention. Spanish and Portuguese speakers may note that the searches are not grammatically correct, but this is as searches do not need to be grammatically correct, and the masculine form will also find the feminine form of nouns and adjectives.

11 These figures were obtained on May 24, 2024. Results on other dates are likely to be different as the database grows.

12 Chin and Morimoto (2013, 98) make a similar call for "greater contextualization" but using different terms.

13 As Harrington (2023) notes, the term "modern games" is "contentious" but is a convenient shorthand for the sorts of games that have been produced in the last thirty years or so. It excludes classic games like Go or Chess or *Xiangqi* (Chinese Chess). See also Booth (2021, 5–6) for a discussion of modern games' popularity.

14 While Harrington doesn't mention it, one wonders what effect the role of colonialism in such games (Flanagan and Jakobsson 2023) has in a postcolonial city like Hong Kong. Booth (2021, 179) argues that the way such games play can position players in "culturally insensitive ways." There is not space in this chapter to go into this discussion in depth, though it is relevant to how fandom develops.

15 Translations from Spanish in this chapter are our own unless otherwise stated.

16 https://www.youtube.com/@BoardiesGames.

17 See here for the use of "filler": https://boardgamegeek.com/thread/3155215/filler-games-recommendations. The categories of board game on Board Game Geek are here: https://boardgamegeek.com/browse/boardgamecategory. Categories for non-specialists can be found in this example: https://www.gamesradar.com/best-board-games/.

18 https://www.youtube.com/watch?v=2D5CvQO4k6Y.

19 https://www.youtube.com/watch?v=mDgDnTV101M.

Chapter 4

1 https://www.youtube.com/watch?v=kymDzCgPwj0.

2 In this chapter, we use an inclusive understanding of "queer" to include all non-heteronormative sexualities, following David M. Halperin's argument that queer could be used by "anyone who is or who feels marginalized because of [their] sexual practices" (1995, 62).

3 David Halperin (2012) examines the codes and practices of gay male culture in the United States, for example.

4 There are many other scholars working on queer cinema we could mention here but due to lack of space, we cannot provide a full overview.

5 Though not everywhere, as many countries censor LGBTQIA+ content.

6 Such as the slash based on *Queer as Folk* (Busse and Lothian 2018, 123–4).

7 Similar, as we noted in the previous chapter, to how American fan practices have become viewed as the hegemonic forms.

8 This video "Stictor 看TGCF 英配版 S2 Ep1 reaction, 这台词真是有过而无不及" (Stictor watching TGCF English dubbed version S2 Ep1 reaction, this line is really over the top.) is taken from https://www.bilibili.com/video/BV1Nv411c7mk/?spm_id_from=333.999.0.0&vd_source=0e29afd94a162c74635151e2fb683fac. All discussions about this video, including the translation and viewers' comments, are accessed via this link unless specified otherwise.

9 A popular Chinese platform for disseminating and consuming literary works, mainly novels, by amateur writers.

10 The novel was officially translated into English and published by Seven Seas Entertainment in eight volumes, with the first released in December 2021 and the last in November 2023.

11 The comics was also published by Bilibili in 2019 and its English translation was accessible through Bilibili Comics Channel before the channel was shut down in February 2024.

12 This data is based on a search of the title TGCF on Netflix via Unofficial Netflix Online Global Search (UNoGS), a search engine collecting information regarding the availability of a title on the Netflix platform in different regions and languages.

13 We should note that the subtitles differ from the words spoken here, as sometimes happens in fan translation as the subtitler may have misheard.

14 At the time of writing, that is, August 2024.

Chapter 5

1 The Translators Association in the UK currently recommends a price of £100 per thousand words (*c.* US$130 per thousand words). A 50,000-word novel, then, would cost £5,000

(*c.* $6,600). The website of the Translators Association can be found here: https://www2.societyofauthors.org/groups/translators-association/.

2 It seems to us there is some interesting overlap between retro gaming fandom—that is, the fandom of 8 and 16 bit consoles such as the PC Engine and Megadrive or home computers like the C64 and Amiga—and romhacking, but we do not have space to explore this in the current book.

3 Venuti (2019) theorizes this understanding of translation as opposed to a more interpretive form of translation.

4 See van der Meer (2023) for more recent considerations of how large language models are affecting the translation industry.

5 While stressing the human here, we are also aware of the more complex, more-than-human network of elements in reading that have been discussed in recent critical theory (e.g., Snaza 2019). However, in the face of AI and algorithms, we feel it is important to continue to recognize the importance of human agency in the creation and circulation of cultural artifacts.

6 Kim, Choi, and Evans (2023, 322) mention the failure of HERMES but do not offer any analysis of the case.

7 For example, the general guidelines are here: https://partnerhelp.netflixstudios.com/hc/en-us/articles/215758617-Timed-Text-Style-Guide-General-Requirements.

8 We checked this using Norwegian, like the Netflix example. The translations were "gjorde et drap," *did a murder* and "må ut på veien" *have to [go] out to the road.* The second is closer to the idiomatic meaning if still too literal.

9 For a discussion of international subtitling practices on Netflix, see Pedersen (2018). Standard subtitling practices are discussed by Díaz-Cintas and Remael (2021). Orrego-Carmona (2016) finds that audiences do not always perceive the differences in quality between professional and amateur subtitles.

10 *Danmaku* is Japanese; they are also known as *danmu* in Chinese.

11 On the theoretical fecundity of wildness, see Halberstam and Nyong'o (2018).

REFERENCES

Altman, Dennis. 2001. *Global Sex*. Chicago: University of Chicago Press.

Amaral, Adriana, Libertad Borda, Nadiezhda Camacho Quiroz, and Clarice Greco. 2024. "Fan Studies in Latin America: A Call to Arms." Translated by Gianlluca Simi. *Transformative Works and Cultures*, no. 43. https://doi.org/10.3983/twc.2024.2689.

Ameri, Saeed, and Masood Khoshsaligheh. 2019. "Iranian Amateur Subtitling Apparatus: A Qualitative Investigation." *Mutatis Mutandis: Revista Latinoamericana de Traducción* 12, no. 2: 433–53. https://doi.org/10.17533/udea.mut.v12n2a05.

Anthony, Sebastian. 2017. "Fansubs for TV Shows and Movies Are Illegal, Court Rules." *Ars Technica*, April 21. https://arstechnica.com/tech-policy/2017/04/fan-made-subtitles-for-tv-shows-and-movies-are-illegal/.

Antonini, Rachele, and Chiara Bucaria, eds. 2016. *Non-Professional Interpreting and Translation in the Media*. Bern: Lang.

Antonini, Rachele, Letizia Cirillo, Linda Rossato, and Ira Torresi, eds. 2017. *Non-Professional Interpreting and Translation*. Amsterdam: Benjamins.

Apter, Emily. 2013. *Against World Literature: On the Politics of Untranslatability*. London: Verso.

Arenas-Castro, Henry, Violeta Berdejo-Espinola, Shawan Chowdhury, Argelia Rodríguez-Contreras, Aubrie R. M. James, Nussaïbah B. Raja, Emma M. Dunne, Sandro Bertolino, Nayara Braga Emidio, Chantelle M. Derez, et al. 2024. "Academic Publishing Requires Linguistically Inclusive Policies." *Proceedings of the Royal Society B: Biological Sciences* 291: 20232840. https://doi.org/10.1098/rspb.2023.2840.

Azuma, Hiroki. 2009. *Otaku: Japan's Database Animals*. Translated by Jonathan E. Able and Shion Kono. Minneapolis: University of Minnesota Press.

Bacon-Smith, Camille. 1992. *Enterprising Women: Television Fandom and the Creation of Popular Myth*. Philadelphia: University of Pennsylvania Press.

Baer, Brian James. 2020. "On Origins: The Mythistory of Translation Studies and the Geopolitics of Knowledge." *The Translator* 26, no. 3: 221–40. https://doi.org/10.1080/13556509.2020.1843755.

Baer, Brian James. 2021. *Queer Theory and Translation Studies: Language, Politics, Desire.* Abingdon: Routledge.

Baer, Brian James, and Klaus Kaindl, eds. 2018. *Queering Translation, Translating the Queer: Theory, Practice, Activism.* Abingdon: Routledge.

Baldo, Michaela, Jonathan Evans, and Ting Guo, eds. 2021. *Translation and LGBT/Queer Activism.* Special issue of *Translation and Interpreting Studies* 16, no. 2: 185–324.

Baldo, Michaela, Jonathan Evans, and Ting Guo, eds. 2023. *Translating the Queer Popular.* Special issue of *Perspectives* 31, no. 2: 165–281.

Baetens, Jan. 2018. *Novelization: From Film to Novel.* Columbus: The Ohio State University Press.

Báez, Jillian M. 2018. "Charting Latinx Fandom." In *The Routledge Companion to Media Fandom*, edited by Melissa A. Click and Suzanne Scott, 271–9. New York: Routledge.

Baker, Mona, ed. 2016. *Translating Dissent: Voices from and within the Egyptian Revolution.* Abingdon: Routledge.

Banks, John, and Mark Deuze. 2009. "Co-Creative Labour." *International Journal of Cultural Studies* 12, no. 5: 419–31. https://doi.org/10.1177/1367877909337862.

Baños, Rocío, and Jorge Díaz-Cintas. 2023. "Exploring New Forms of Audiovisual Translation in the Age of Digital Media: Cybersubtitling and Cyberdubbing." *The Translator* 30, no. 4: 129–44. https://doi.org/10.1080/13556509.2023.2274119.

Barra, Luca. 2009. "The Mediation Is the Message: Italian regionalization of US TV Series as Co-creational Work." *International Journal of Cultural Studies* 12, no. 5: 509–25. https://doi.org/10.1177/1367877909337859.

Bassnett, Susan. 2014. *Translation.* Abingdon: Routledge.

Bassnett, Susan, and Peter Bush, eds. 2006. *The Translator as Writer.* London: Continuum.

Bassnett, Susan, and André Lefevere. 1998. *Constructing Cultures: Essays on Literary Translation.* Clevedon: Multilingual Matters.

Baudinette, Thomas. 2023. *Boys' Love Media in Thailand: Celebrity, Fans, and Transnational Asian Queer Popular Culture.* London: Bloomsbury.

Baugher, Janée J. 2020. *The Ekphrastic Writer: Creating Art-Influenced Poetry, Fiction and Nonfiction.* Jefferson, NC: McFarland.

Bennett, Karen. 2007. "Epistemicide! The Tale of a Predatory Discourse." *The Translator* 13, no. 2: 151–69. https://doi.org/10.1080/13556509.2007.10799236.

Bennett, Lucy, and Paul Booth, eds. 2016. *Seeing Fans: Representations of Fandom in Media and Popular Culture.* London: Bloomsbury.

Berlant, Lauren, and Michael Warner. 1998. "Sex in Public." *Critical Inquiry* 24, no. 2: 547–66. https://doi.org/10.1086/448884.

Biguenet, John, and Rainer Schulte, eds. 1989. *The Craft of Translation.* Chicago, IL: University of Chicago Press.

Binnie, Jon. 2004. *The Globalization of Sexuality.* London: Sage.

Bond, Esther. 2018. "Why Netflix Shut Down Its Translation Portal Hermes." *Slator*, October 19. https://slator.com/why-netflix-shut-down-its-translation-portal-hermes/.

Booth, Paul. 2018. "Board Gamers as Fans." In *The Routledge Companion to Media Fandom*, edited by Melissa A. Click and Suzanne Scott, 428–36. New York: Routledge.

Booth, Paul. 2021. *Board Games as Media.* London: Bloomsbury.

Booth, Paul, and Lucy Bennett. 2016. "Introduction: Seeing Fans." In *Seeing Fans: Representations of Fandom in Media and Popular Culture*, edited by Lucy Bennett and Paul Booth, 1–9. London: Bloomsbury.

Borodo, Michał. 2022. "Non-Professional Translators and the Media." In *The Routledge Handbook of Translation and Media*, edited by Esperança Bielsa, 432–45. Abingdon: Routledge.

Brennan, Joseph, ed. 2019. *Queerbaiting and Fandom: Teasing Fans through Homoerotic Possibilities.* Iowa City: University of Iowa Press.

Brienza, Casey. 2016. *Manga in America: Transnational Book Publishing and the Domestication of Japanese Comics.* London: Bloomsbury.

Briggs, Kate. 2017. *This Little Art.* London: Fitzcarraldo.

Busse, Kristina, and Alexis Lothian. 2018. "A History of Slash Sexualities: Debating Queer Sex, Gay Politics and Media Fan Cultures." In *The Routledge Companion to Media, Sex and Sexuality*, edited by Clarissa Smith and Feona Attwood with Brian McNair, 117–29. Abingdon: Routledge.

Casanova, Pascale. 1999. *La République mondiale des lettres*. Paris: Seuil.

Chachu, Sewoenam, and Luke Liebzie, eds. 2023. *Community Translation and Interpreting in Africa*. Special issue of *Journal for Translation Studies in Africa*, 5: 1–83. https://doi.org/10.38140/jtsa.v5i.

Chan, Leo Tak-Hung. 2010. *Readers, Reading and the Reception of Translated Fiction in Chinese*. Manchester: St Jerome.

Chan, Leo Tak-Hung. 2012. "A Survey of the 'New' Discipline of Adaptation Studies: Between Translation and Interculturalism." *Perspectives* 20, no. 4: 411–18. https://doi.org/10.1080/0907676X.2012.726232.

Chang, Jie, and Gang Zhao. 2022. "The Reader's Visibility: Analyzing Reader's Intervention in Fan-Based Translation on Wuxiaworld." *Translation Review* 113, no. 1: 33–47. https://doi.org/10.1080/07374836.2022.2089414.

Chao, Shih-chen. 2017. "Cosplay, Cuteness, and *Weiniang*: The Queered *ke'ai* of Male Cosplayers as 'Fake Girls'." In *Boy's Love, Cosplay and Androgynous Idols: Queer Fan Cultures in Mainland China, Hong Kong, and Taiwan*, edited by Maud Lavin, Ling Yang, and Jing Jamie Zhao, 20–44. Hong Kong: Hong Kong University Press.

Chaturvedi, Rahul, Hariom Singh, and Anita Singh, eds. 2021. *Hero and Hero-Worship: Fandom in Modern India*. Wilmington, DE: Vernon Press.

Chaume, Federic. 2012. *Audiovisual Translation: Dubbing*. Manchester: St Jerome.

Chen, Zhen Troy, and Celia Lam, eds. 2023. *Chinese Fandoms*. Special issue of *Transformative Works and Cultures*, no. 41. https://doi.org/10.3983/twc.2023.2627.

Chen, Yue, Qin Gao, and Pei-Luen Patrick Rau. 2017. "Watching a Movie Alone yet Together: Understanding Reasons for Watching Danmaku Videos." *International Journal of Human–Computer Interaction* 33, no. 9: 731–43. http://doi.org/10.1080/10447318.2017.1282187.

Chin, Bertha. 2007. "Beyond Kung-Fu and Violence: Locating East Asian Cinema Fandom." In *Fandom: Identities and Communities in a Mediated World*, edited by Jonathan Gray, Cornel Sandvoss, and C. Lee Harrington, 210–19. New York: New York University Press.

Chin, Bertha, and Lori Hitchcock Morimoti. 2013. "Towards a Theory of Transcultural Fandom." *Participations* 10, no. 1: 92–108. https://www.participations.org/10-01-07-chin.pdf.

Chin, Bertha, Aswin Punathambekar, and Sangita Shresthova. 2018. "Advancing Transcultural Fandom: A Conversation." In *The Routledge Companion to Media Fandom*, edited by Melissa A. Click and Suzanne Scott, 298–306. New York: Routledge.

Choi, Jinsil, Kyung Hye Kim, and Jonathan Evans. 2023. "Introduction: Translation and Streaming in a Changing World." *Target* 35, no. 3: 319–30. https://doi.org/10.1075/target.00020 .cho.

Ciecko, Anne, and Hunju Lee. 2007. "Han Suk-kyu and the Gendered Cultural Economy of Stardom and Fandom." In *Fandom: Identities and Communities in a Mediated World*, edited by Jonathan Gray, Cornel Sandvoss, and C. Lee Harrington, 220–31. New York: New York University Press.

Click, Melissa A., and Suzanne Scott, eds. 2018. *The Routledge Companion to Media Fandom*. New York: Routledge.

Collier, Noelle R., Christine A. Lumadue, and H. Ray Wooten. 2009. "*Buffy the Vampire Slayer* and *Xena: Warrior Princess*: Reception of the Texts by a Sample of Lesbian Fans and Web Site Users." *Journal of Homosexuality* 56, no. 5: 575–609. https://doi .org/10.1080/00918360903005253.

Consalvo, Mia. 2016. *From Atari to Zelda: Japan's Videogames in Global Contexts*. Cambridge, MA: MIT Press. https://doi.org/10 .7551/mitpress/8853.001.0001.

Coupland, Nikolas. 2009. *Language, Identity and Performance: Sociolinguistic Perspectives on Wales*. Cardiff: University of Wales Press.

Crisp, Virginia. 2015. *Film Distribution in the Digital Age: Pirates and Professionals*. Basingstoke: Palgrave Macmillan.

Cronin, Michael. 2013. *Translation in the Digital Age*. Abingdon: Routledge.

Cruz, Angela Gracia B., Yuri Seo, and Itar Binay. 2021. "Cultural Globalization from the Periphery: Translation Practices of English K-pop Fans." *Journal of Consumer Culture* 21, no. 3: 638–59. https://doi.org/10.1177/1469540519846215.

Curran, James, and Myung-Jin Park, eds. 2000. *De-Westernizing Media Studies*. London: Routledge.

Dale, Pete. 2012. *Anyone Can Do It: Empowerment, Tradition and the Punk Underground*. London: Ashgate.

Danforth, Emily. M. 2012. *The Miseducation of Cameron Post*. New York: Balzer + Bray.

DeAngelis, Michael. 2001. *Gay Fandom and Crossover Stardom: James Dean, Mel Gibson, and Keanu Reeves*. Durham, NC: Duke University Press.

Declercq, Christophe, and Gys-Walt van Egdom. 2023. "No More Buying Cats in a Bag? Literary Translation in the Age of Automation." *Revista Tradumàtica* 21: 49–62. https://doi.org/10.5565/rev/tradumatica.407.

Denison, Rayna. 2011. "Anime Fandom and the Liminal Spaces between Fan Creativity and Piracy." *International Journal of Cultural Studies* 14, no. 5: 449–66. https://doi.org/10.1177/1367877910394565.

Denison, Rayna. 2015. *Anime: A Critical Introduction*. London: Bloomsbury.

Deppey, Dirk. 2005. "Scanlation Nation: Amateur Manga Translators Tell Their Stories." *Comics Journal*, no. 269: 33–5. http://archives.tcj.com/269/n_scan.html.

Derrida, Jacques. 1992. "From *Des Tours de Babel*." Translated by Joseph F. Graham. In *Theories of Translation: An Anthology of Essays from Dryden to Derrida*, edited by Rainer Schulte and John Biguenet, 218–27. Chicago, IL: University of Chicago Press.

Deuze, Mark. 2007. *Media Work*. Cambridge: Polity.

Deuze, Mark, Catherine Tosenberger, Jordan Greenhall, Elizabeth Osder, and Raph Koster. 2007. "Futures of Entertainment 2: 'Fan Labor'." *MIT Comparative Media Studies* [Podcast]. https://cms.mit.edu/fan-labor/.

Díaz-Cintas, Jorge, and Pablo Muñoz Sánchez. 2006. "Fansubs: Audiovisual Translation in an Amateur Environment." *Journal of Specialised Translation* 6: 37–52. https://jostrans.soap2.ch/issue06/art_diaz_munoz.pdf.

Díaz-Cintas, Jorge, and Aline Remael. 2021. *Subtitling: Concepts and Practices*. Abingdon: Routledge.

Díaz-Cintas, Jorge, Pablo Muñoz Sánchez, and Willian Henrique Cândido Moura. 2022. "Fansubs: Tradução Audiovisual em um Ambiente Amador." *Cadernos De Tradução* 42, no. 1: 1–26. https://doi.org/10.5007/2175-7968.2022.e80264.

Driver, Susan. 2007. *Queer Girls and Popular Culture: Reading, Resisting, and Creating Media*. New York: Lang.

Duggan, Jennifer, and Angie Fazekas. 2023. "Trans Fandom" [editorial]. In "Trans Fandom," edited by Jennifer Duggan and Angie Fazekas, Special issue, *Transformative Works and Cultures*, no. 39. https://doi.org/10.3983/twc.2023.2521.

Dwyer, Tessa. 2012. "Fansub Dreaming on Viki: 'Don't Just Watch but Help When You Are Free'." *The Translator* 18, no. 2: 217–43. https://doi.org/10.1080/13556509.2012.10799509.

Dwyer, Tessa. 2017. *Speaking in Subtitles: Revaluing Screen Translation*. Edinburgh: Edinburgh University Press.

Dwyer, Tessa. 2018. "Audiovisual Translation and Fandom." In *The Routledge Handbook of Audiovisual Translation*, edited by Luis Pérez-González, 436–52. Abingdon: Routledge.

Eco, Umberto. 2003. *Mouse or Rat? Translation as Negotiation*. London: Phoenix.

Eng, David L., Judith Halberstam, and José Esteban Muñoz. 2005. "Introduction: What's Queer About Queer Studies Now?" *Social Text* 23, nos. 3–4: 1–17.

Epstein, B. J., and Robert Gillett, eds. 2017. *Queer in Translation*. Abingdon: Routledge.

Evans, Jonathan. 2013. "Translating Board Games: Multimodality and Play." *Journal of Specialised Translation* 20: 15–32. https://jostrans.soap2.ch/issue20/art_evans.pdf.

Evans, Jonathan. 2020a. "Fan Translation." In *Routledge Encyclopedia of Translation Studies*, 3rd ed., edited by Mona Baker and Gabriela Saldanha, 177–81. Abingdon: Routledge.

Evans, Jonathan. 2020b. "Translation, Accessibility and Variation in Global Analog Gaming." *Analog Game Studies* 7, no. 1. https://analoggamestudies.org/2020/03/translation-accessibility-and-variation-in-global-analog-gaming/.

Evans, Jonathan. 2022. "Media Studies." In *Routledge Handbook of Translation and Methodology*, edited by Federico Zanettin and Chris Rundle, 78–93. Abingdon: Routledge.

Eve, Martin Paul. 2016. "'You Have to Keep Track of Your Changes': The Version Variants and Publishing History of David Mitchell's *Cloud Atlas*." *Open Library of Humanities* 2, no. 2: e1. https://doi.org/10.16995/olh.82.

Fabbretti, Matteo. 2015. "Manga Scanlation for an International Readership: The Role of English as a lingua franca." *The*

Translator 23, no. 4: 456–73. https://doi.org/10.1080/13556509
.2017.1385938.

Fabian, Dorottya. 2015. *A Musicology of Performance: Theory and
Method Based on Bach's Solos for Violin*. Cambridge: Open
Book Publishers.

Ferrer Simó, María Rosario. 2005. "Fansubs y scanlations: la
influencia del aficionado en los criterios profesionales." *Puentes*
6: 27–44. https://wpd.ugr.es/~greti/revista-puentes/pub6/04-Maria
-Rosario-Ferrer.pdf.

Felski, Rita. 2020. *Hooked: Art and Attachment*. Chicago, IL:
University of Chicago Press.

Fettner, Chris, and Denny Sheehan. 2017a. "Netflix is Looking
for the Best Translators Around the Globe." *Netflix*, March 30.
https://about.netflix.com/en/news/netflix-is-looking-for-the-best
-translators-around-the-globe.

Fettner, Chris, and Denny Sheehan. 2017b. "The Netflix HERMES
Test: Quality Subtitling at Scale." *Netflix Technology Blog*,
March 30. https://netflixtechblog.com/the-netflix-hermes-test
-quality-subtitling-at-scale-dccea2682aef.

Fiske, John. 1989. *Understanding Popular Culture*. London: Unwin
Hyman.

Fish, Stanley. 1982. *Is There a Text in This Class? The Authority of
Interpretive Communities*. Cambridge, MA: Harvard University
Press.

Flanagan, Mary, and Mikael Jakobsson. 2023. *Playing Oppression:
The Legacy of Conquest and Empire in Colonialist Board
Games*. Cambridge, MA: MIT Press.

Flaubert, Gustave. 2011. *Madame Bovary: Provincial Ways*.
Translated by Lydia Davis. London: Penguin.

Flood, Alison. 2016. "Translated Fiction Sells Better in the UK than
English Fiction, Research Finds." *The Guardian*, May 9. https://
www.theguardian.com/books/2016/may/09/translated-fiction
-sells-better-uk-english-fiction-elena-ferrante-haruki-murakami.

Friedman, Erica. 2017. "On Defining Yuri." In *Queer Female
Fandom*, edited by Julie Levin Russo and Eve Ng, Special issue,
Transformative Works and Cultures, no. 24. http://dx.doi.org/10
.3983/twc.2017.831.

Gottlieb, Henrik. 1994. "Subtitling: Diagonal Translation."
Perspectives 2, no. 1: 101–21. doi:10.1080/09076
76X.1994.9961227.

Gramling, David, and Aniruddha Dutta, eds. 2016. *Translating Transgender*. Special issue of *Transgender Studies Quarterly* 3, nos. 3–4: 331–636.

Gauntlett, David. 2018. *Making is Connecting: The Social Power of Creativity, from Craft and Knitting to Digital Everything*, 2nd ed. Cambridge: Polity.

Gray, Jonathan. 2010. *Show Sold Separately: Promos, Spoilers, and other Media Paratexts*. New York: New York University Press.

Gray, Jonathan, Cornel Sandvoss, and C. Lee Harrington, eds. 2007. *Fandom: Identities and Communities in a Mediated World*. New York: New York University Press.

Guo, Ting. 2021. "'Love is Love' and 'Love is Equal', Fansubbing and Queer Feminism in China." In *Translating Feminism: Interdisciplinary Approaches to Text, Place and Agency*, edited by Maud Ann Bracke, Julia C. Bullock, Penelope Morris, and Kristina Schulz, 199–226. Basingstoke: Palgrave Macmillan.

Guo, Ting, and Jonathan Evans. 2020. "Translational and Transnational Queer Fandom in China: The Fansubbing of *Carol*." *Feminist Media Studies* 20, no. 4: 515–29. http://doi.org/10.1080/14680777.2020.1754630.

Halberstam, Jack, and Tavia Nyong'o. 2018. "Introduction: Theory in the Wild." *South Atlantic Quarterly* 117, no. 3: 453–64. https://doi.org/10.1215/00382876-6942081.

Halperin, David M. 1995. *Saint Foucault: Towards a Gay Hagiography*. Oxford: Oxford University Press.

Halperin, David M. 2012. *How to Be Gay*. Cambridge, MA: Belknap Press.

Hampton, Darlene. 2016. "Slashy Rotten Pervs: Transnational Media Representations of *Sherlock* Slash Fans and the Politics of Pathologization." In *Seeing Fans: Representations of Fandom in Media and Popular Culture*, edited by Lucy Bennett and Paul Booth, 229–38. London: Bloomsbury.

Han, Benjamin. 2017. "K-Pop in Latin America: Transcultural Fandom and Digital Mediation." *International Journal of Communication* 11: 2250–69. https://ijoc.org/index.php/ijoc/article/view/6304/2048.

Harrington, J. 2023. "Let's Meetup? Board Game Communities in Hong Kong." *Games and Culture* 20, no. 3: 279–97. https://doi.org/10.1177/15554120231202707.

Harvey, Keith. 1998. "Translating Camp Talk: Gay Identities and Cultural Transfer." *The Translator* 4, no. 2: 295–320. https://doi.org/10.1080/13556509.1998.10799024.

Harvey, Keith. 2003. *Intercultural Movements: American Gay in French Translation*. Manchester: St Jerome.

Hatcher, Jordan S. 2005. "Of Otaku and Fansubs: A Critical Look at Anime Online in Light of Current Issues in Copyright Law." *Script-ed* 2, no. 4: 545–71. https://papers.ssrn.com/sol3/papers.cfm?abstract_id=871098.

Hayes, Joseph J. 1976. "Gayspeak." *Quarterly Journal of Speech* 62, no. 3: 256–66. https://doi.org/10.1080/00335637609383340.

Henthorn, Jamie. 2019. "International Fan Professionalization on Viki." *Television & New Media* 20, no. 5: 525–38. https://doi.org/10.1177/1527476418770742.

Hesmondhalgh, David. 2010. "User-Generated Content, Free Labour and the Cultural Industries." *Ephemera: Theory and Politics in Organization* 10, nos. 3–4: 267–84. https://ephemerajournal.org/contribution/user-generated-content-free-labour-and-cultural-industries.

Hills, Matt. 2002. *Fan Cultures*. London: Routledge.

Hills, Matt. 2005. *How to Do Things with Cultural Theory*. London: Hodder Arnold.

Hills, Matt. 2017. "Transnational Cult and/as Neoliberalism: The Liminal Economies of Anime Fansubbers." *Transnational Cinemas* 8, no. 1: 80–94. https://doi.org/10.1080/20403526.2016.1245921.

Hogan, Heather. 2016. "The 'Carol' Oscars Snub: The Problem Isn't Lesbians. It's Misandry." *Autostraddle.com*, January 14. https://www.autostraddle.com/carol-didnt-get-oscar-snubbed-because-its-too-gay-it-got-oscar-snubbed-because-it-dismisses-men-324022/.

Hu, Kelly. 2013. "Competition and Collaboration: Chinese Video Websites, Subtitle Groups, State Regulation and Market." *International Journal of Cultural Studies* 17, no. 5: 437–51. https://doi.org/10.1177/1367877913505170.

Hutcheon, Linda. 2006. *A Theory of Adaptation*. Abingdon: Routledge.

Iwabuchi, Koichi. 2002. *Recentering Globalization: Popular Culture and Japanese Transnationalism*. Durham, NC: Duke University Press.

Jakobson, Roman. 2012. "On Linguistic Aspects of Translation." In *The Translation Studies Reader*, 3rd ed., edited by Lawrence Venuti, 126–31. Abingdon: Routledge.

Jenkins, Henry. 1992. *Textual Poachers: Television Fans and Participatory Culture*. London: Routledge.

Jenkins, Henry. 2006a. *Fans, Bloggers, and Gamers: Exploring Participatory Culture*. New York: New York University Press.

Jenkins, Henry. 2006b. *Convergence Culture: Where Old and New Media Collide*, updated ed. New York: New York University Press.

Jenkins, Henry, Sam Ford, and Joshua Green. 2013. *Spreadable Media: Creating Value and Meaning in a Networked World*. New York: New York University Press.

Jenkins, Henry, Sangita Shresthova, Liana Gamber-Thompson, Neta Kligler-Vilenchik, and Arely Zimmerman. 2016. *By Any Media Necessary: The New Youth Activism*. New York: New York University Press.

Jin, Haina, and Zijin Ye. 2022. "Translating Queer Elements in *Bohemian Rhapsody* in China." *Perspectives* 31, no. 2: 187–204. https://doi.org/10.1080/0907676X.2022.2105155.

Kaross, Luciana, and Renata Spinola. 2012. "'Words Which Could Only be Your Own': The Crossroad Between Lyrics Translation, Culture, Brazilian Fans, and Non-Professional Translators." *Revista Vozes dos Vales* 2: 1–17. http://site.ufvjm.edu.br/revista multidisciplinar/files/2011/09/Words-which-could-only-be-your -own_the-crossroad-between-lyrics-translation-culture-Brazilian -fans-and-non-professional-translators_luciana-1.pdf.

Keenaghan, Eric. 1998. "Jack Spicer's Pricks and Cocksuckers: Translating Homosexuality into Visibility." *The Translator* 4, no. 2: 273–94. https://doi.org/10.1080/13556509.1998 .10799023.

Kelly, William W., ed. 2004. *Fanning the Flames: Fans and Consumer Culture in Japan*. Albany: State University of New York Press.

Kennedy, David, and Richard Meek, eds. 2018. *Ekphrastic Encounters: New Interdisciplinary Essays on Literature and the Visual Arts*. Manchester: Manchester University Press.

Kenny, Dorothy. 2018. "Sustaining Disruption? The Transition from Statistical to Neural Machine Translation." *Revista Tradumàtica* 16: 59–70. https://doi.org/10.5565/rev/tradumatica.221.

Kustritz, Anne, ed. 2015. *European Fans and European Fan Objects: Localization and Translation*. Special issue of *Transformative Works and Cultures*, no. 19.

Lakarnchua, Onuma. 2017. "Examining the Potential of Fansubbing as a Language Learning Activity." *Innovation in Language Learning and Teaching* 11, no. 1: 32–44. http://doi.org/10.1080/17501229.2015.1016030.

Lamerichs, Nicolle. 2016. "Otaku: Representations of Fandom in Japanese Popular Culture." In *Seeing Fans: Representations of Fandom in Media and Popular Culture*, edited by Lucy Bennett and Paul Booth, 251–62. London: Bloomsbury.

Lange, Anne, Daniele Monticelli, and Chris Rundle, eds. 2024. *The Routledge Handbook of the History of Translation Studies*. Abingdon: Routledge.

Lavin, Maud, Ling Yang, and Jing Jamie Zhao, eds. 2017. *Boys' Love, Cosplay, and Androgynous Idols: Queer Fan Cultures in Mainland China, Hong Kong, and Taiwan*. Hong Kong: Hong Kong University Press.

Lee, Benjamin. 2024. "I Saw the TV Glow Review—Devastating Tale of Identity, Fandom and Obsession." *The Guardian*, January 20. https://www.theguardian.com/film/2024/jan/20/i-saw-the-tv-glow-review-devastating-tale-of-identity-and-obsession.

Lee, Hye-Kyung. 2009. "Between Fan Culture and Copyright Infringement: Manga Scanlation." *Media, Culture & Society* 31, no. 6: 1011–22. https://doi.org/10.1177/0163443709344251.

Lee, Hye-Kyung. 2011. "Cultural Consumer and Copyright: A Case Study of Fansubbing Anime." *Creative Industries Journal* 3, no. 3: 237–52. https://doi.org/10.1386/cij.3.3.237_1.

Lee, Tong King. 2020. "Translation and Copyright: Towards a Distributed View of Originality and Authorship." *The Translator* 26, no. 3: 241–56. https://doi.org/10.1080/13556509.2020.1836770.

Lefevere, André. 1992. *Translating, Rewriting and the Manipulation of Literary Fame*. London: Routledge.

Leonard, Sean. 2005. "Progress Against the Law: Anime and Fandom, with the Key to Globalization of Culture." *International Journal of Cultural Studies* 8, no. 3: 281–305. https://doi.org/10.1177/1367877905055679.

Li, Dang. 2021. "The Transcultural Flow and Consumption of Online *Wuxia* Literature through Fan-Based Translation."

Interventions 23, no. 7: 1041–65. https://doi.org/10.1080 /1369801X.2020.1854815.

Lionnet, Françoise, and Shu-mei Shih. 2005. "Introduction: Thinking through the Minor, Transnationally." In *Minor Transnationalism*, edited by Françoise Lionnet and Shu-mei Shih, 1–23. Durham, NC: Duke University Press.

Llamas, Carmen, and Dominic Watt, eds. 2009. *Language and Identities*. Edinburgh: University of Edinburgh Press.

Luczaj, Kamil, Magdalena Holy-Luczaj, and Karolina Cwiek-Rogalska. 2014. "Fansubbers: The Case of the Czech Republic and Poland." *Journal of Comparative Research in Anthropology and Sociology* 5, no. 2: 175–98. http://compaso.eu/wpd/wp -content/uploads/2015/02/Compaso2014-52-Luczaj-et-al.pdf.

Luong, Van Nhan, and Jonathan Evans. 2021. "Fan Translation in the Vietnamese Context: A Preliminary Study." *Asia Pacific Translation and Intercultural Studies* 8, no. 2: 163–77. http://doi .org/10.1080/23306343.2021.1931782.

Madeley, June. M. 2015. "Transnational Convergence Culture: Grassroots and Corporate Convergence in the Conflict Over Amateur English-Translated Manga." *Journal of Graphic Novels and Comics* 6, no. 4: 367–81. https://doi.org/10.1080/21504857.2015 .1060617.

Madill, Anna. 2018. "Erotic Manga: Boys' Love, *shonen-ai*, *yaoi* and (MxM) *shotacon*." In *The Routledge Companion to Media, Sex and Sexuality*, edited by Clarissa Smith and Feona Attwood with Brian McNair, 130–40. Abingdon: Routledge.

Madrid-Morales, Dani, and Bruno Lovric. 2015. "'Transatlantic Connection': K-pop and K-drama Fandom in Spain and Latin America." *Journal of Fandom Studies* 3, no. 1: 23–41. https://doi .org/10.1386/jfs.3.1.23_1.

Magazzù, Giulia. 2023. "When We Rise: Comparing the Official Italian Dubbing and the Fansubs of a LGBT Docu-Series." *Perspectives* 31, no. 2: 205–19. https://doi.org/10.1080 /0907676X.2022.2038928.

Mandelin, Clyde. 2013. "Fan Translation: Does It Help or Hurt Getting Professional Work?" *Legends of Localization*, November 3. https://legendsoflocalization.com/fan-translation-does-it-help -or-hurt-getting-professional-work/.

Martin, Fran. 2017. "Girls Who Love Boys' Love: BL as Goods to Think with in Taiwan." In *Boys' Love, Cosplay and*

Androgynous Idols: Queer Fan Cultures in Mainland China, Hong Kong, and Taiwan, edited by Maud Lavin, Ling Yang, and Jing Jamie Zhao, 195–219. Hong Kong: Hong Kong University Press.

Martínez Pleguezuelos, Antonio J. 2018. *Traducción e identidad sexual: Reescrituras audiovisuals desde la Téoria Queer*. Granada: Comares.

Massad, Joseph Andoni. 2002. "Re-Orienting Desire: The Gay International and the Arab World." *Public Culture* 14, no. 2: 361–85. muse.jhu.edu/article/26284.

Massidda, Serenella. 2015. *Audiovisual Translation in the Digital Age: The Italian Fansubbing Phenomenon*. Basingstoke: Palgrave Macmillan.

McKee, Alan. 2007. "The Fans of Cultural Theory." In *Fandom: Identities and Communities in a Mediated World*, edited by Jonathan Gray, Cornel Sandvoss, and C. Lee Harrington, 88–97. New York: New York University Press.

Mertens, Jacob. 2023. "Abridged Anime and the Distance in Fan-Dubbing: Interpreting Culture Through Parody and Fan Appropriation." *International Journal of Cultural Studies* 26, no. 2: 182–99. https://doi.org/10.1177/13678779221145439.

Mignolo, Walter D. 2012. *Local Histories/Global Designs: Coloniality, Subaltern Knowledges, and Border Thinking*. Princeton, NJ: Princeton University Press.

Milton, John, and Silvia Cobelo. 2023. *Translation, Adaptation and Digital Media*. Abingdon: Routledge.

Min, Wonjung, Dal Yong Jin, and Benjamin Han. 2019. "Transcultural Fandom of the Korean Wave in Latin America: Through the Lens of Cultural Intimacy and Affinity Space." *Media, Culture & Society* 41, no. 5: 604–19. https://doi.org/10.1177/0163443718799403.

Mitchell, David. 2004. *Cloud Atlas*. London: Sceptre.

Morimoto, Lori Hitchcock. 2016. "The Good Fandom: Depicting Japanese Fans in Moonlight Express, Moumantai, and Hong Kong Star Fans." In *Seeing Fans: Representations of Fandom in Media and Popular Culture*, edited by Lucy Bennett and Paul Booth, 239–50. London: Bloomsbury.

Morozov, Evgeny. 2011. *The Net Delusion: How Not to Liberate the World*. London: Penguin.

Moura Aragão, Sabrina. 2016. "Scanlatione o poder do leitor-autor na tradução de mangás." *TradTerm* 27: 75–113. https://doi.org /10.11606/issn.2317-9511.v27i0p75-113.

Munday, Jeremy, Sara Ramos Pinto, and Jacob Blakesley. 2022. *Introducing Translation Studies: Theories and Applications*, 5th ed. Abingdon: Routledge.

Mundim, Isabella Santos. 2001. "Roswell, Textual Gaps and Fan's Subversive Response." *Cadernos De Tradução* 1, no. 7: 229–45. https://doi.org/10.5007/%x.

Muñoz Sánchez, Pablo. 2008. "En torno a la localización de videojuegos clásicos mediante técnicas de romhacking: particularidades, calidad y aspectos legales." *Journal of Specialised Translation* 9: 80–95. http://www.jostrans.org/issue09 /art_munoz_sanchez.php.

Muñoz Sánchez, Pablo. 2009. "Video Game Localization by Fans for Fans: The Case of Romhacking." *The Journal of Internationalization and Localization* 1, no. 1: 168–85. https:// doi.org/10.1075/jial.1.07mun.

Nagaike, Kazumi, and Katsuhiko Suganuma. 2013. "Transnational Boys' Love Fan Studies [editorial]." *Transformative Works and Cultures*, no. 12. https://doi.org/10.3983/twc.2013.0504.

Newman, James. 2018. "Kaizo Mario Maker: ROM Hacking, Abusive Game Design and Nintendo's Super Mario Maker." *Convergence* 24, no. 4: 339–56. https://doi.org/10.1177 /1354856516677540.

Ng, Eve. 2017. "Between Text, Paratext, and Context: Queerbaiting and the Contemporary Media Landscape." In "Queer Female Fandom," edited by Julie Levin Russo and Eve Ng, Special issue, *Transformative Works and Cultures*, no. 24. http://dx.doi.org/10 .3983/twc.2017.917.

Ng, Eve. 2023. *Mainstreaming Gays: Critical Convergences of Queer Media, Fan Cultures, and Commercial Television*. New Brunswick, NJ: Rutgers University Press.

Ng, Eve, and Julie Levin Russo. 2017. "Envisioning Queer Female Fandom." *Transformative Works and Cultures*, no. 24. http://dx .doi.org/10.3983/twc.2017.1168.

Ng, Eve, and Xiaomeng Li. 2020. "A Queer 'Socialist Brotherhood': The *Guardian* Web Series, Boys' Love Fandom, and the Chinese State." *Feminist Media Studies* 20, no. 4: 479–95. http://dx.doi .org/10.1080/14680777.2020.1754627.

Ngai, Sianne. 2012. *Our Aesthetic Categories: Zany, Cute, Interesting*. Cambridge, MA: Harvard University Press.

Nord, Christiane, Masood Khoshsaligheh, and Saeed Ameri. 2015. "Socio-Cultural and Technical Issues in Non-expert Dubbing: A Case Study." *International Journal of Society, Culture & Language* 3, no. 2: 1–16. https://www.ijscl.com/article_11734 _b9fac3605ffb0c68da832760430a527b.pdf.

Nornes, Abé Mark. 1999. "For an Abusive Subtitling." *Film Quarterly* 53, no. 3: 17–34. https://doi.org/10.2307/1213822.

Nornes, Abé Mark. 2007. *Cinema Babel: Translating Global Cinema*. Minneapolis: University of Minnesota Press.

Nunes Viera, Lucas, Elise Alonso, and Lindsay Bywood. 2019. "Introduction: Post-Editing in Practice—Process, Product and Networks." *Journal of Specialised Translation* 31: 2–23. https:// jostrans.soap2.ch/issue31/art_introduction.pdf.

O'Hagan, Minako. 2008. "Fan Translation Networks: An Accidental Translator Training Environment." In *Translator and Interpreter Training: Issues, Methods and Debates*, edited by John Kearns, 158–83. London: Continuum.

O'Hagan, Minako. 2009. "Evolution of User-generated Translation: Fansubs, Translation Hacking and Crowdsourcing." *The Journal of Internationalization and Localization* 1, no. 1: 94–121. https:// doi.org/10.1075/jial.1.04hag.

O'Hagan, Minako. 2016. "Massively Open Translation: Unpacking the Relationship Between Translation and Technology in the 21st Century." *International Journal of Communication* 10: 929–46. https://ijoc.org/index.php/ijoc/article/view/3507.

O'Hagan, Minako, and Carmen Mangiron. 2013. *Game Localization: Translating for the Global Digital Entertainment Industry*. Amsterdam: Benjamins.

Orrego-Carmona, David. 2016. "A Reception Study on Non-Professional Subtitling: Do Audiences Notice Any Difference?" *Across Languages and Cultures* 17, no. 2: 163–81. http://doi.org /10.1556/084.2016.17.2.2.

Orrego-Carmona, David, and Yvonne Lee, eds. 2017. *Non-Professional Subtitling*. Newcastle-upon-Tyne: Cambridge Scholars.

Pande, Rukmini. 2016. "Squee from the Margins: Racial/Cultural/ Ethnic Identity in Global Media Fandom." In *Seeing Fans:*

Representations of Fandom in Media and Popular Culture, edited by Lucy Bennett and Paul Booth, 209–20. London: Bloomsbury.

Pande, Rukmini. 2018. *Squee from the Margins: Fandom and Race.* Iowa City: University of Iowa Press.

Pappen, Paulo Henrique. 2023. "Tradução e Teatro Amador: Conceitos de uma Pesquisa Prática." *Cadernos de Tradução* 43, no. 1: 218–35. https://doi.org/10.5007/2175-7968.2023.e92134.

Pedersen, Jan. 2018. "From Old Tricks to Netflix: How Local are Interlingual Subtitling Norms for Streamed Television?" *Journal of Audiovisual Translation* 1, no. 1: 81–100. https://doi.org/10.47476/jat.v1i1.46.

Pedersen, Jan. 2019. "Fansubbing in Subtitling Land: An Investigation Into the Nature of Fansubs in Sweden." *Target* 31, no. 1: 50–76. https://doi.org/10.1075/target.18017.ped.

Pérez-González, Luis. 2006. "Fansubbing Anime: Insights into the 'Butterfly' Effects of Globalisation on Audiovisual Translation." *Perspectives* 14, no. 4: 260–77. https://doi.org/10.1080/09076760708669043.

Pérez-González, Luis. 2014. *Audiovisual Translation: Theories, Methods and Issues.* Abingdon: Routledge.

Pérez-González, Luis. 2020. "Fan Audiovisual Translation." In *Routledge Encyclopedia of Translation Studies*, 3rd ed., edited by Mona Baker and Gabriela Saldanha, 172–7. Abingdon: Routledge.

Pérez-González, Luis, and Şebnem Susam-Saraeva. 2012. "Non-Professionals Translating and Interpreting: Participatory and Engaged Perspectives." *The Translator* 18, no. 2: 149–65. https://doi.org/10.1080/13556509.2012.10799506.

Pickles, Matthew. 2018. "K-pop Drives Boom in Korean Language Lessons." *BBC*, July 11. https://www.bbc.co.uk/news/business-44770777.

Pillière, Linda. 2021. *Intralingual Translation of British Novels: A Multimodal Stylistic Analysis.* London: Bloomsbury.

Pillière, Linda, and Özlem Berk Albachten, eds. 2024. *The Routledge Handbook of Intralingual Translation.* Abingdon: Routledge.

Powell, Ryan. 2019. *Coming Together: The Cinematic Elaboration of Gay Male Life, 1945–1979.* Chicago, IL: University of Chicago Press.

Prieto-Rodríguez, Juan, and Víctor Fernández-Blanco. 2000. "Are Popular and Classical Music Listeners the Same People?" *Journal*

of *Cultural Economics* 24: 147–64. https://doi.org/10.1023/A
:1007620605785.

Punathambekar, Aswin. 2007. "Between Rowdies and *Rasikas*:
Rethinking Fan Activity in Indian Film Culture." In *Fandom:
Identities and Communities in a Mediated World*, edited by
Jonathan Gray, Cornel Sandvoss, and C. Lee Harrington,
198–209. New York: New York University Press.

Pym, Anthony. 2004. *The Moving Text: Localization, Translation,
and Distribution*. Amsterdam: Benjamins.

Pym, Anthony. 2023. *Exploring Translation Theories*, 3rd ed.
Abingdon: Routledge.

Ramírez, David. 2017. "La biblioteca del aficionado pobre: José
Lezama Lima y la (de)formación por la lectura." *Mutatis
Mutandis: Revista Latinoamericana de Traducción* 10, no. 1:
70–85. https://doi.org/10.17533/udea.mut.327036.

Raw, Laurence, ed. 2012. *Translation, Adaptation and
Transformation*. London: Bloomsbury.

Ricketson, Sam, and Jane Ginsburg, eds. 2022. *International
Copyright and Neighbouring Rights: The Berne Convention and
Beyond*, 3rd ed. Oxford: Oxford University Press.

Robinson, Douglas. 2019. *Translation, Transgender, Translingual
Address*. London: Bloomsbury.

Ruh, Brian. 2010. "Transforming U.S. Anime in the 1980s:
Localization and Longevity." In *Mechademia 5: Fanthropologies*,
31–49. Minneapolis: University of Minnesota Press.

Sakamoto, Akiko, Jonathan Evans, and Olga Torres Hostench. 2018.
"Introduction to the Special Dossier Section 'Translation and
Disruption'." *Revista Tradumàtica* 16: 52–8. https://doi.org/10
.5565/rev/tradumatica.223.

Sakai, Naoki. 2006. "Translation." *Theory, Culture & Society* 23,
nos. 2–3: 71–8. https://doi.org/10.1177/0263276406063778.

Sandvoss, Cornel. 2005. *Fans: The Mirror of Consumption*.
Cambridge: Polity.

Savcı, Evren. 2021. *Queer in Translation: Sexual Politics Under
Neoliberal Islam*. Durham, NC: Duke University Press.

Schules, Douglas. 2014. "How to Do Things with Fan Subs: Media
Engagement as Subcultural Capital in Anime Fan Subbing."
Transformative Works and Cultures 17. https://doi.org/10.3983/
twc.2014.0512.

Scott, Clive. 2000. *Translating Baudelaire*. Exeter: University of Exeter Press.

Sedgwick, Eve Kosofsky. 1994. *Tendencies*. London: Routledge.

Sennett, Richard. 2008. *The Craftsman*. London: Penguin.

Shafirova, Liudmila, and Daniel Cassany. 2019. "Bronies Learning English in the Digital Wild." *Language Learning & Technology* 23, no. 1: 127–44. https://doi.org/10125/44676.

Shih, Shu-mei, and Françoise Lionnet. 2011. "Introduction: The Creolization of Theory." In *The Creolization of Theory*, edited by Françoise Lionnet, and Shu-mei Shih, 1–33. Durham, NC: Duke University Press.

Shohat, Ella, and Robert Stam. 1994. *Unthinking Eurocentrism: Multiculturalism and the Media*. London: Routledge.

Snaza, Nathan. 2019. *Animate Literacies: Literature, Affect and the Politics of Humanism*. Durham, NC: Duke University Press.

Spencer, Amy. 2008. *DIY: The Rise of Lo-fi Culture*. London: Marion Boyars.

Spurlin, William, ed. 2014. *The Gender and Queer Politics of Translation: Literary, Historical and Cultural Approaches*. Special issue of *Comparative Literature Studies* 51, no. 2: 201–367. https://doi.org/10.5325/complitstudies.51.2.fm.

Stanfill, Mel. 2019. *Exploiting Fandom: How the Media Industry Seeks to Manipulate Fans*. Iowa City: University of Iowa Press.

Susam-Saraeva, Şebnem. 2015. *Translation and Popular Music: Transcultural Intimacy in Turkish-Greek Relations*. Bern: Lang.

Tachtiris, Corinne. 2024. *Translation and Race*. Abingdon: Routledge.

Terranova, Tiziana. 2000. "Free Labor: Producing Culture for the Digital Economy." *Social Text* 18, no. 2: 33–58. muse.jhu.edu/article/31873.

Terranova, Tiziana. 2022. *After the Internet: Digital Networks between Capital and the Common*. South Pasadena, CA: Semiotext(e).

Three Percent. n.d. "About." *Three Percent*. https://www.rochester.edu/College/translation/threepercent/about/.

Tremblay, Alyssa. 2018. "Found in Translation: Rethinking the Relationship Between Fan Translation Groups and Licensed Distributors of Anime and Manga." *Journal of Fandom Studies* 6, no. 3: 319–33. https://doi.org/10.1386/jfs.6.3.319_1.

Trykowska, Natalia. 2009. "Manga Scanlation in Poland." *Translation Ireland* 18, no. 1: 5–24.

Tulloch, John. 2007. "Fans of Chekov: Re-Approaching 'High Culture'." In *Fandom: Identities and Communities in a Mediated World*, edited by Jonathan Gray, Cornel Sandvoss, and C. Lee Harrington, 110–22. New York: New York University Press.

TWC Editor. 2023. "Fan Studies State of the Field 2023." *Transformative Works and Cultures*, no. 40. https://doi.org/10 .3983/twc.2023.2593.

Uribe-Jongbloed, Enrique. 2020. "Playing with Translation: Translanguaging Role-Playing Games in Colombia in the 1990s." *Analog Game Studies* 7, no. 1. https://analoggamestudies.org /2020/03/playing-with-translation-translanguaging-role-playing -games-in-colombia-in-the-1990s/.

Vaidhyanathan, Siva. 2001. *Copyrights and Copywrongs: The Rise of Intellectual Property and How It Threatens Creativity*. New York: New York University Press.

van der Meer, Jaap. 2023. "AI Revolution Changes the Translation Industry." *TAUS*, 16 May. https://www.taus.net/resources/blog/ai -revolution-changes-the-translation-industry.

Van der Sar, Ernesto. 2017. "Founder of Fan-Made Subtitle Site Convicted for Copyright Infringement." *Torrent Freak*. https:// torrentfreak.com/founder-of-subtitle-site-convicted-for-copyright -infringement-170914/.

van Doorslaer, Luc, and Peter Flynn, eds. 2013. *Eurocentrism in Translation Studies*. Amsterdam: Benjamins.

Vazquez-Calvo, Boris. 2021. "Guerrilla Fan Translation, Language Learning, and Metalinguistic Discussion in a Catalan-Speaking Community of Gamers." *ReCALL* 33, no. 3: 296–313. https://doi .org/10.1017/S095834402000021X.

Venuti, Lawrence. 1995. *The Translator's Invisibility*. London: Routledge.

Venuti, Lawrence. 2019. *Contra Instrumentalism: A Translation Polemic*. Lincoln: University of Nebraska Press.

Wang, Dingkun. 2017. "Fansubbing in China—with Particular Reference to the Fansubbing Group YYETS." *Journal of Specialised Translation*, no. 28: 165–88. https://jostrans.soap2.ch/ issue28/art_wang.pdf.

Wang, Dingkun. 2022. "Chinese Translational Fandoms: Transgressing the Distributive Agency of Assemblages in

Audiovisual Media." *International Journal of Cultural Studies* 25, no. 6: 655–72. https://doi.org/10.1177/13678779221102974.

Wang, Dingkun, and Xiaochun Zhang. 2017. "Fansubbing in China: Technology-Facilitated Activism in Translation." *Target* 29, no. 2: 301–18. https://doi.org/10.1075/target.29.2.06wan.

Wang, Erika Ningxin, and Liang Ge. 2023. "Fan Conflicts and State Power in China: Internalised Heteronormativity, Censorship Sensibilities, and Fandom Police." *Asian Studies Review* 47, no. 2: 355–73. https://doi.org/10.1080/10357823.2022.2112655.

Wanzo, Rebecca. 2015. "African American Acafandom and Other Strangers: New Genealogies of Fan Studies." *Transformative Works and Cultures* 20. https://doi.org/10.3983/twc.2015.0699.

Warner, Kristen J. 2018. "(Black Female) Fans Strike Back: The Emergence of the Iris West Defense Squad." In *The Routledge Companion to Media Fandom*, edited by Melissa A. Click and Suzanne Scott, 253–61. New York: Routledge.

Welker, James, ed. 2023. *Queer Transfigurations: Boys Love Media in Asia*. Honolulu: University of Hawai'i Press.

Whatling, Clare. 1997. *Screen Dreams: Fantasising Lesbians in Film*. Manchester: Manchester University Press.

White, Patricia. 1999. *Uninvited: Classical Hollywood Cinema and Lesbian Representability*. Bloomington: Indiana University Press.

Wittgenstein, Ludwig. 1958. *Philosophical Investigations*. Translated by G. E. M. Anscombe. Oxford: Blackwell.

Wongseree, Thandao, Minako O'Hagan, and Ryoko Sasamoto. 2019. "Contemporary Global Media Circulation Based on Fan Translation: A Particular Case of Thai Fansubbing." *Discourse, Context & Media* 32: 100330. https://doi.org/10.1016/j.dcm.2019.100330.

Woo, Benjamin. 2018. "The Invisible Bag of Holding: Whiteness and Media Fandom." In *The Routledge Companion to Media Fandom*, edited by Melissa A. Click and Suzanne Scott, 245–52. New York: Routledge.

Wu, You. 2021. "Revisiting Translation in the Age of Digital Globalization: The 'Going Global' of Chinese Web Fiction Through Overseas Volunteer Translation Websites." *Babel* 67, no. 6: 819–44. https://doi.org/10.1075/babel.00248.wu.

Xinhua. 2021. "Chinese Police Arrest 14 for Running Pirated-video Platform YYeTs.com." *XinhuaNet*. http://www.news.cn/english/2021-02/03/c_139718452.htm.

Yang, George. 2021. "Why Japanese Games Are Increasingly Releasing at the Same Time Across the Globe." *IGN*, October 5. https://www.ign.com/articles/why-japanese-games-are -increasingly-releasing-at-the-same-time-across-the-globe.

Yang, Ling, and Xanrui Xu. 2017. "Chinese *danmei* Fandom and Cultural Globalization From Below." In *Boy's Love, Cosplay and Androgynous Idols: Queer Fan Cultures in Mainland China, Hong Kong, and Taiwan*, edited by Maud Lavin, Ling Yang, and Jing Jamie Zhao, 3–19. Hong Kong: Hong Kong University Press.

Yang, Yuhong. 2020. "The Danmaku Interface on Bilibili and the Recontextualised Translation Practice: A Semiotic Technology Perspective." *Social Semiotics* 30, no. 2: 254–73. http://doi.org/10 .1080/10350330.2019.1630962.

Zhang, Charlie Yi. 2017. "When Feminist Falls in Love with Queer: Dan Mei Culture as a Transnational Apparatus of Love." *Feminist Formations* 29, no. 2: 121–46. https://doi.org/10.1353/ ff.2017.0019.

Zhang, Leticia-Tian, and Boris Vazquez-Calvo. 2022. "'¿Triste estás? I don't know nan molla': Multilingual pop song fandubs by @ miree_music." *ITL—International Journal of Applied Linguistics* 173, no. 2: 197–227. https://doi.org/10.1075/itl.21007.zha.

Zhang, Shanshan. 2022. "Exploring How Chinese TV Dramas Reach Global Audiences via Viki in the Transnational Flow of TV Content." *Journal of Transcultural Communication* 2, no. 1: 69–89. https://doi.org/10.1515/jtc-2022-0014.

Zhang, Weiyu, and Chengting Mao. 2013. "Fan Activism Sustained and Challenged: Participatory Culture in Chinese Online Translation Communities." *Chinese Journal of Communication* 6, no. 1: 45–61. https://doi.org/10.1080/17544750.2013 .753499.

Zhao, Jamie J. 2021. "Introduction: Global Queer Fandoms of Asian Media and Celebrities." *Feminist Media Studies* 21, no. 6: 1028–32. https://doi.org/10.1080/14680777.2021.1959374.

Zhao, Jing Jamie, Ling Yang, and Maud Lavin. 2017. "Introduction." In *Boys' Love, Cosplay, and Androgynous Idols: Queer Fan Cultures in Mainland China, Hong Kong, and Taiwan*, edited by Lavin Maud, Ling Yang, and Jamie Jing Zhao, xi– xxxiii. Hong Kong: Hong Kong University Press.

Zheng, Xiqing. 2024. "Chinese Media Production and Fandom Between Queerbaiting and 'Survival Instincts'." *Media,*

Culture & Society 46, no. 7: 1437–53. https://doi.org/10.1177/01634437241241964.

Zhu, Ying. 2023. "The Therapeutic and the Transgressive: Chinese Fansub Straddling between Hollywood IP Laws and Chinese State Censorship." *Global Storytelling: Journal of Digital and Moving Images* 3, no. 1: 2. https://doi.org/10.3998/gs.4293.

Zollner, Amelia. 2023. "Major Publishers Report That Aaa Franchises Can Cost Over a Billion to Make." *IGN*, April 29. https://www.ign.com/articles/major-publishers-report-aaa-franchises-can-cost-over-a-billion-to-make.

Zwischenberger, Cornelia. 2022. "Online Collaborative Translation: Its Ethical, Social, and Conceptual Conditions and Consequences." *Perspectives* 30, no. 1: 1–18. https://doi.org/10.1080/0907676X.2021.1872662.

INDEX